ALL THINGS POSSIBLE

ALL THINGS POSSIBLE

How to Definitely Experience Inner Peace, Spiritual Growth and the Fulfillment of Life's Purposes

ROY EUGENE DAVIS

CSA PRESS, *Publishers*   Lakemont, Georgia 30552

Copyright © 1991 by Roy Eugene Davis

ISBN 0-87707-231-0

Material from this book may be freely quoted for reviews, articles and other purposes, with credit given to title and author.

CSA PRESS, *Publishers*
Post Office Box 7
Lake Rabun Road
Lakemont, Georgia 30552 (U.S.A.)

CSA PRESS is the educational literature department of Center for Spiritual Awareness in Lakemont, Georgia.

For individual orders in West Africa: Center for Spiritual Awareness, Post Office Box 507, Accra, Ghana; Peter Oye Agencies, Post Office Box 5803, Lagos, Nigeria. In Europe: Verlag Marco Del Nero, Postfach 1471, D-6350 Bad Nauheim 1, Germany.

Distributed in New Zealand by Peaceful Living Publications, Post Office Box 300, Tauranga B.O.P.; and in Great Britain by L.N. Fowler and Company, Ltd., 1201 High Road, Chadwell Heath, Romford, Essex RM6 4DH

PRINTED IN THE UNITED STATES OF AMERICA

*I salute the supreme teacher,
the Truth,
whose nature is bliss,
who is the giver of the highest
happiness,
who is beyond all qualities
and infinite like the sky,
who is beyond words,
who is one and eternal,
pure and still,
who is beyond all change
and phenomena,
and who is the silent witness
to all our thoughts and emotions;
I salute Truth,
the supreme teacher.*
[*From an Ancient Vedic Hymn*]

THE AUTHOR

Roy Eugene Davis is internationally known for his clear exposition of conscious living principles, with books published in five languages and a frequent lecture schedule to major U.S. cities and several countries.

Born 1931 in Ohio, he began his spiritual training with Paramahansa Yogananda in 1950 in Los Angeles, California. He is presently the director of Center for Spiritual Awareness, with headquarters and retreat center in Lakemont, Georgia, and branches in several U.S. cities, Europe and West Africa.

INTRODUCTION

What is it, that will satisfy the heart's sincere desire? Nothing ephemeral will, because temporary interludes of sensory and emotional satisfaction but remind us of the impermanence of objects, relationships and circumstances. What every person (every spiritual being) wants, is soul satisfaction that results from knowledge, spiritual growth and evidence that life's purposes are being experienced and fulfilled.

Why is it, that while we inwardly know this to be true, so few among the world's increasing population are really happy, really fulfilled, really at peace within themselves and with the natural order? Is it because of widespread ignorance of the facts of life? Frequently, yes. But with the increasing availability of knowledge, we must look elsewhere for the cause.

The primary cause of spiritual dissatisfaction is absence of burning soul desire to experience spiritual growth. This is why I say that *any rational person can definitely experience inner peace, spiritual growth and the fulfillment of life's purposes, if he or she sincerely wants to.*

Is the process easy? It can be, if the way is known and one will cooperate with it. It may also be challenging; yet not to choose the higher way is to continually meet with challenges of the most impossible kind, as well as to miss out of life's great adventure—that of growing to maturity and experiencing expanded states of consciousness which, coincidently, result in understanding and its corresponding soul-liberating outcomes.

While this book was but a concept in my mind, I mailed

a questionnaire form to about 4 thousand persons and invited their response. Approximately 500 forms were sent back* and what was shared is much appreciated by me, and was extremely helpful as the project progressed.

Almost all of the respondents declared a belief in God. Many affirmed a conviction of the continuity of life and several stated a belief in reincarnation, at least as a possibility. Many also described experiences they had which, to them, indicated sometimes supernatural intervention in their lives. Also described were occasional episodes of a paranormal character: such as out-of-body experiences, precognitive dreams, telepathy, and what seemed to them to be valid communication with deceased relatives and friends.

A common challenge reported by many was that of learning to let go of self-limiting (and sometimes self-destructive) attitudes, beliefs and behaviors assumed or adopted years earlier. Money was not reported to be much of a problem, although some said they could use more. Physical illness or distress was mentioned by only a few. Many expressed genuine concern about social and planetary conditions.

Since the questionnaire purposely did not request that respondents identify themselves by name, it is believed that the information shared was forthright and honest.

The fast-awakening world in which we presently live provides us the opportunity for learning, growth and service. Almost six billion human beings are alive today, with a quarter of a million increase being added every 24 hours. Scientific discoveries and technological advances are contributing to our fund of this-world knowledge as

* Respondents represented a fair sampling of societal circumstances. The majority were of middle-age, while many were young adults and a few were in their seventies and eighties. Some were retired. A few were jobless. Most were actively working, their occupations varied. Secretaries, medical doctors, chiropractors, sales representatives, airplane pilots and cabin attendants, nurses, school teachers, college professors, policemen, factory workers, ministers, business owners, working mothers, radio and television broadcasters, and factory workers were included.

well as challenging us to probe the accessible boundaries which converge between objective and subjective realms—between the world as we perceive it and the subtle and fine realms which are its cause and support. The discoveries of a few, challenge the minds of the many and fairly invite an expansion of consciousness and a more aware, responsible approach to living if the world-as-it-is-becoming-known is to be related to with understanding. Personal outer circumstances can be changed or adapted to according to desire and need, while the great essential remains that of our being focused on a life-path which is, for us, the one best suited to spiritual growth and the fulfillment of destiny.

If you care about yourself, other people and your world, read and *use* this book! As you proceed, refer to a dictionary if necessary to ensure comprehension of word meanings. If a sentence or a theme is not clear to you, review it until it is. Use the recommended procedures and planning guides in order to enter fully into the processes of learning and practice. As you proceed, you will discover that there is a benevolent Power which nourishes you (and everyone else) and that as you cooperate with it to allow It to fulfill Its purposes, your needs are met and your worthy purposes are more easily fulfilled.

I know who, and what you are: You are a spiritual being with virtually unlimited capacities, because you are grounded in the Infinite. I know you are capable of experiencing inner peace, spiritual growth and the fulfillment of life's purposes because, at the inmost level of your being...you sincerely want to.

Roy Eugene Davis
Lakemont, Georgia
April 17, 1991

Contents

Introduction / 7

One: Life's Purposes and Inner Peace

Life's purposes and inner peace / 15
The four primary aims of human life to
 understand and actualize / 20
What prevents us from expressing our innate
 knowledge and creativity? / 22
How to definitely experience useful changes in
 lifestyle and psychological and spiritual growth / 25
The spiritual basis of inner peace / 28
Living can be natural, enjoyable and spontaneous / 33
Psychological and spiritual growth can be natural,
 enjoyable and spontaneous / 35
How to have the courage to live and be fulfilled / 38
Why all human problems must (and do) have a
 spiritual solution / 42
Prospering can be natural, enjoyable and
 spontaneous / 48
On waking up, growing up and facing up to reality / 60
Extending awareness beyond the boundaries of mind
 and senses / 66
Miracles are in the eye of the beholder / 71

Two: Living in God

Living in God / 75
The one relationship that makes all others
 worthwhile / 76
The primary importance of complete spiritual
 education for every person / 79
How can we know what is true? / 81
God, the world and us / 82

How to walk and talk with God / 85
But, what about the evil in the world? / 94
How to pray, with results following / 99
What happens when we die to this world? / 102
The seven levels of soul awareness that determine
    perceptions, behavior and experience / 110
Righteousness and grace: learning to let God to it / 114

Three: Your Personalized Program

Your personalized program for definitely experiencing
    inner peace, spiritual growth and the fulfillment of
    life's purposes / 125
Consciously choose a lifestyle fully supportive of
    your worthy purposes and spiritual growth / 128
Meditate for personal benefits and accelerated
    spiritual growth / 130
Imagine all the possibilities / 136
If you need healing, do these things / 141
Your body is the temple in which God dwells / 146
The one hour a day that can anchor your life in
    the Infinite / 151
Be good to the universe and the universe will be good
    to you / 153
Write your possible futures, with love / 154
Form # 1: Your Life Mission Statement / 157
Form # 2: Write Your Hopes and Dreams / 159
Form # 3: Specific Program for Spiritual Growth / 160
Form # 4: Your "one hour a day" Self-Care Routine / 163
Form # 5: Physical Wellness and Vitality Program / 164
Form # 6: Enjoyable Life-Enhancing Activities / 166
Form # 7: Worthy Projects to be Actualized / 167
Form # 8: Cultivating a Prosperity Consciousness / 168
Form # 9: A Comprehensive Life-Plan / 170
Form #10: An Affirmation of All Things Possible / 172

Epilogue

Answers to Often Asked Questions / 175

ONE

Life's Purposes and Inner Peace

The divine voice was always in their ears. Often they misunderstood it. Or they thought they heard it when it was only the echo of their own thoughts and wishes they had heard; but the desire to hear it, the sense that life consisted in hearing it, —that never left them.
PHILLIPS BROOKS (1835-1893)
Sermons

Henceforth, please God, forever I forgo
The yoke of men's opinions. I will be
Light-hearted as a bird, and live with
    God.
I find him in the bottom of my heart.
I hear continually his voice therein.

The little needle always knows the North,
The little bird remembereth his note,
And the wise Seer within me never errs.
I never taught it what it teaches me;
I only follow when I act aright.
RALPH WALDO EMERSON
Self-Reliance

Life's purpose is growth and fulfillment. Therefore, your purpose, and my purpose, is growth and fulfillment.

The plain, simple truth is that we are not in this world merely to exclusively attend to personal egocentric interests and to satisfy every mood-inspired whim and emotionally motivated desire. We were not born only to eat, cope, procreate, respond to every sensory urge, and die. Even death is not the end of the journey for us, for we will continue to live, be challenged to learn and grow to maturity and eventually awaken to an understanding of life's processes after we have departed this realm.

We have choices. We can choose to remain as we are, in whatever conditions may be presently experienced. We can choose to withdraw from present circumstances by dramatizing a variety of neurotic or psychotic symptoms. We can choose to avoid responsible behavior, and the learning opportunities it provides, by indulging in obsessive behavior or by being addicted to drugs, alcohol or other escape routines. We can even wish we were dead, and perhaps consciously or unconsciously contrive to arrange this condition. Or we can choose to educate ourselves, learn how to live successfully, consider life as a great adventure and joyfully experience it. Sooner or later, the latter way is the one that will have to be accepted because the urgency of evolution will not permit any other permanent choice.

So what is life all about, anyway? What is the reason for the universe and the incessant transformations it undergoes? What is our role in the cosmic process? What is expected of us? What is God doing, through us and through and, as, the universe? If there are answers to these and other reasonable questions, why are they not commonly known? And if it is true that we are spiritual beings "made in the image and likeness of God," why is it that we do not clearly know this and why can we not express our innate divinity? Honest answers to these honest questions will be offered in this text and I assure you that if you want to, you can discover them for yourself.

The purpose of life, this side of the point of creation (or manifestation) is to express. Evidence of this is that life *is* expressing throughout the universe, at fine and subtle levels in the subatomic realms and at the more obvious levels we are able to perceive through our senses. Our role (and we would do well to learn to appreciate it) is to learn, to grow to emotional and spiritual maturity, and to find out how to consciously and willingly participate in life's processes. Along with our own growth, we are here to serve the cause of evolution. Let us be very clear about this—God and the universe do not exist to serve us (although we are served by God and the universe), we are here to serve God and life's purposes. In fact, it is more accurate to say "God *as* the universe" rather than "God *and* the universe" because God-as-energy *is* manifesting *as* the universe. We will examine this occurrence and, together, better understand it, in the following portions of this book.

God's will and life's purposes are one and the same: the transformation of matter and the spiritual awakening of souls. It is well for us to understand this if we have chosen to definitely experience inner peace, spiritual growth, and the fulfillment of life's purposes because these ends cannot be realized by agreeing, at the same time, to live out of conditioned states of consciousness and confused mental states. They cannot be realized by compulsive behavior or by well intentioned but misguided personal effort.

When we are growing emotionally and spiritually, when we are in the flow of life and serving as we are meant to serve, we are happy. When we are not growing, when

Life's Purposes and Inner Peace

we are not progressively experiencing expanded states of consciousness, when we are not in harmony with evolutionary processes and the rhythms of Nature, we are unhappy. True happiness is soul satisfaction because of comprehensive understanding and the doing of what we are meant to do. The only real satisfaction is peace of soul and this is only established when we are consciously surrendered in the understanding, and experience, of our permanent nature. Our permanent nature is being. When awareness is overly involved with mental transformations (thought processes, imagery, and the continual shifting of attitudes and moods) and with sensory perceptions, confusion results. The outer becomes more obvious than the inner. Awareness becomes confined and restricted, instead of being unbounded or universal, which is its natural state.

Every soul's destiny is to awaken to a condition of God-consciousness. Awakening may be gradual and progressive, or it may be instantaneous, but the latter event is uncommon. Usually, soul awakening is experienced as quite ordinary shifts of consciousness: from simple states of consciousness to self-consciousness, then to higher states referred to as superconsciousness and degrees of cosmic consciousness prior to God-consciousness. This eventual conclusion is not the result of experiences that we have: our experiences reflect our progressive changes in states of consciousness, because states of consciousness (our degrees of awareness, therefore our capacity to comprehend and perform) determine mental states and behavior.

As an example, we may desire to be more functional and to behave more reasonably than we do, but be unable to do so because of being fixed at a level of awareness from which self-determined behavior is difficult to implement. Sometimes this inner resistance to useful changes in attitude and behavior is palpable. It is so obvious that we can perceive it as a seemingly independent force exerting influence contrary to our will. The result may be that, as the years go by, we will confess that "We have left undone those things which we ought to have done; And we have done those things which we ought not to have done*." Yet, when we do extend and involve ourselves in appropriate, intentional ways we soon discover that a benevolent force more real than the inner resistances becomes increasingly influential in its drive to contribute to our higher understanding and more constructive behavior. We discover that soul capacities awaken and become increasingly influential, that available grace becomes increasingly evident.

Spiritual awakening can be neglected, avoided for a while, even denied as being necessary, but it cannot forever be suppressed. Adventuresome, healthy-minded people will welcome this evolutionary growth-process with enthusiasm and think it to be quite a splendid outcome. Egocentric people may resist, or fear, its implications. Apathetic people may give it little consideration, or even possibly disavow the existence of God or any evidence of evolutionary influences in their, or anyone else's lives.

But think about it!—if this is our certain destiny (and it is), what are we doing to contribute to its culmination? *One of the most amazing facts about the human condition, which is almost incredible when we think about it, is that the single most important discovery we can ever make— that of who and what we really are, and what our relationship to the universe is—is almost totally unknown and unexperienced by the majority of people on Earth today!*

To bring the matter of life's purposes into focus, so that we can involve ourselves with intention and consciously participate in cooperating with these purposes, let's examine our choices in relationship to opportunities and responsibilities. Regardless of our present means of attempting to satisfy our innate urge to be happy, let us understand that this urge is really our inclination to be fully conscious and unrestricted. Because this is a primary drive, it will continue to be a motivating influence until it is actualized. Any neglect, any attempt at avoid-

---

* *The Book of Common Prayer* [1928], "A General Confession," page 6.

Life's Purposes and Inner Peace

ance of our inevitable spiritual growth, is but a feeble effort to put off what will, sooner or later, occur. The opening lines of the poem by Francis Thompson* immediately portray the situation:

> I fled Him, down the nights and down the days;
> I fled Him, down the arches of the years;
> I fled Him, down the labyrinthine ways
> Of my own mind; and in the midst of tears
> I hid from Him, and under running laughter.

And there is no escape:

> But with unhurrying chase,
> And unperturbed pace,
> Deliberate speed, majestic instancy,
> They beat—and a Voice beat
> More instant than the Feet—
> "All things betray thee, who betrayest Me."

One responsibility we have to ourselves is to learn how to be functional and secure in the universe. This means we have to be knowledgeable about how to relate to it, get along with its inhabitants, and have access to and intelligently use available resources. There are various ways to do these things. There is the difficult way, the easier way, and the easiest way.

The *difficult way* is the way of struggle, the way of coping without attempting to acquire knowledge of how to better proceed. It is the way of force, of expediency without clear understanding of future outcomes, the way of ignorance.

The *easier way* is the way of understanding, experimentation, intelligent use of creative faculties, and of being open to possibilities while learning to contribute to their unfoldment.

The *easiest way* is the way of knowledge and wisdom,

---

* *The Hound of Heaven*, Francis Thompson [1859 – 1907]

cooperation with life's natural inclination to harmoniously unfold, and of learning how to be surrendered to grace.

Because we are spiritual beings, in a spiritual universe (it being a manifestation of God's consciousness and energy) we have virtually unlimited possibilities for expression and experience. The determining factor is: How sincerely do we want to consciously understand this fact and what are we willing to do to help ourselves become more knowledgeable and fully functional?

The Four Primary Aims of Human Life to Understand and Actualize

To experience complete fulfillment there are four major aims of life to be understood and experienced. These provide us with purpose and enable us to fulfill our aspirations.

1. *Acceptance and Fulfillment of Personal Duties* – So long as we relate to the universe we have duties (responsibilities, obligations) to accept and fulfill. We have an obligation to be self-responsible and contribute to our own wellness and function, we have duties in relationship to other human beings and living creatures, and we are responsible for how we relate to and nurture Planet Earth (or whatever sphere might be ours to eventually experience). As we proceed through life there are other obligations that coincide along with the general routines and relationships we might assume. Learning to appropriately perform our duties is not only essential, it is an exceptional exercise in spiritual growth.

2. *The Fulfillment of Legitimate Needs and Desires* – Our legitimate needs and desires are those which are necessary to survival, wellness, function, and the fulfill-

ment of higher purposes. These can include the satisfaction of emotional needs and desires which contribute to our learning and true happiness. It is recommended that one honestly evaluate needs and desires and establish priorities in order to accomplish useful purposes and avoid the waste of effort and resources.

3. *The Willingness to Have an Open Relationship with the Universe* – The universe is more than adequate to meet our needs and to enable us to fulfill our purposes when we learn how to relate to it. We have to be open to our available good fortune, prudently use the resources at hand, and provide for ourselves, and others, a secure lifestyle as well as fulfill our legitimate needs and desires. We can have access to everything we need for comfort and expression when we learn to have an open relationship with the universe. If we cannot learn to have such a relationship, it is unlikely that we will be able to experience emotional and spiritual growth. On the other hand, a degree of spiritual growth will result in improved understanding so that we are more easily able to understand our relationship with the universe.

4. *The Aspiration to be Self-Realized and to Experience God Consciousness* – Without this aspiration we will remain at the level of human consciousness, subject to the influences of mental conditionings and outer circumstances. We may succeed, in some measure, in creating a lifestyle which is comfortable but this will not result in peace of soul. Whether one believes in a future heaven, the doctrine of reincarnation, or that death of the body is the end of existence, life without spiritual growth is purposeless.

The ideal is to attend to all four aspects of life in a balanced, intentional way and do everything possible to contribute to making our sojourn here pleasant and productive. Young people should plan their lives with this perspective. Adults should make necessary changes when insights prompt them to do so. Those in their twilight years who may not have known about these opportunities (or who knew about them but were not as attentive as they could have been) should focus on clearing their consciousness in preparation for the new learning opportunities life will provide in their remaining years and in the hereafter. It is never too soon, or too late, to come to terms with life.

What Prevents Us from Actualizing Our Innate Knowledge and Creativity?

There are two universally prevalent causes of soul restriction and two self-created restrictions. What are they, and how can they be eliminated? Is lack of education a major restricting factor? Are environmental circumstances the problem? Are the emotional traumas we might have accumulated because of past errors in judgment or harsh treatment at the hands of others (or fate) keeping us in bondage? What about karma, the influence of collective consciousness (the thoughts, moods, states of consciousness and behaviors of the almost 6 billion people with whom we share the planet), or political uncertainty and economic conditions?

The *two universally prevalent causes* are the soul's identification with matter and its subsequent forgetfulness of its real nature. This results in delusion, a partially unconscious condition*.

The two *self-created* restricting factors which inhibit spiritual growth and interfere with attempts to accomplish purposes are ones actualized people have renounced or outgrown and which most others refuse to acknowledge even when attention is directed to them. They are *self-centeredness* and *laziness*.

A rational person will acknowledge this fact immediately. A person whose life is based on self-centered behavior and who is lazy, may respond with self-righteous

---

*See the following chapter for a detailed explanation of this occurrence.

indignation!

Self-centeredness is the direct result of *egoism*, and egoism is the condition of feeling ourselves to be independent beings, apart from God and Nature. It is a common problem and there is a solution for it. The way to dissolve egoism is to be more surrendered to life and to extend awareness to more expansive levels in order to experience psychological and spiritual growth.

Self-centered attitudes cause selfish behavior and unrealistic perceptions. A self-centered person almost always projects blame on others, or circumstances, for his misfortune. If assertive, he may attempt to dominate others in obvious, or subtle, ways and may exploit the environment. An obvious effort to dominate is evident when one has a need to control other people. A subtle way is to pretend weakness or incompetence, to whine and complain. (Being habitually late for an agreed upon appointment is often our unconscious way of trying to be in control of circumstances.) Some people habitually get sick, have accidents, overdraw their bank account, or pretend to be unable to learn or comprehend, to protect their psychological condition or attract the attention they crave. A passive self-centered person may become dependent upon relationships and behaviors. A common statement heard from assertive self-centered people is, "I'm going to get what I want, no matter what I have to do to get it!" From passive types one hears, "Why are these unfortunate things always happening to me?"

Laziness, if it does not have a biochemical basis, is a symptom of disinterest, futility, or a reluctance to experience psychological growth. Lazy people make excuses. They rationalize their behavior. They seldom help themselves beyond the level required to survive, or to satisfy personal desires which don't demand too much effort of any kind. Unless a degree of curiosity is present, or partial awakening occurs, a lazy person will waste his life. And a wasted life is a major tragedy.

We might fill pages with descriptions of various contributing causes of restriction and failure, but these would only be categories of conditions stemming from self-righteousness and laziness. I am of course referring here to persons who are reasonably functional and who are not suffering from neurological damage, severe psychological disorders, imbalances of body chemistry, or oppressive environmental circumstances beyond their present control. Even in the latter instance, as soon as one can begin to envision more desirable possibilities, subtle creative forces will become operational to bring about useful changes.

In all instances of human experience various factors are involved. This is concisely explained in the *Bhagavad Gita**:

> Now there are five factors involved in every action: the body, the ego, the deluded soul, that (desire) which initiates the action, and providence. Whatever a person undertakes to do, these five factors are involved. Because of these, if a person thinks that he alone is the doer, he is mistaken.

Whether the body is healthy or unhealthy (functional or impaired) is a factor in actions involving the use of the body. Egoism, or lack of it, determines attitudes, perception, and behaviors. Degrees of delusion (unknowingness) or enlightenment (knowledge) certainly determine behavior. The desire or intention one has determines outcomes, because desires tend to reproduce after their kind. Providence, the manifestation of divine care or direction, is influential, always. It makes possible planned and unplanned good fortune and often contributes to our well-being in spite of our misguided efforts or any other circumstances which may be present.

---

* *Bhagavad Gita* 18: 13, 14

How to Definitely Experience Useful Changes in Lifestyle and Psychological and Spiritual Growth

Should we focus on one need at a time, or should we proceed with plans to implement a more comprehensive program? Do both: solve pressing problems as soon as possible, while simultaneously being involved in programs designed for total wellness, including psychological and spiritual growth. In this way, progress in one area will benefit all others. We are a spirit-mind-body functional unit while in this world, so all levels should be included in regimens used to contribute to balanced unfoldment.

Examples of unbalanced lives are easy to recognize. We may be so focused on "spiritual enlightenment" that attention given to physical health, psychological wellness, supportive relationships, and practical matters relating to financial security and the provision of basic necessities is minimal. We may be so involved with attempts to establish or maintain meaningful relationships that spiritual growth is neglected. Again, we may be so focused on material gain that human relationships deteriorate and spiritual values are ignored. Persons obsessed with chemical, food-related, or other dependencies may be so involved with the problem that hardly any other matter concerns them. Persons involved in long-term psychotherapy may feel that functional living, for them, is but a distant hope or an impossible dream.

The ideal is to adopt a lifestyle that fully supports our higher purposes, provides a foundation for continued growth, and allows for the progressive unfoldment of worthwhile plans. If we are resolved on a spiritual growth path, we definitely should not settle for a lifestyle which conforms to patterns of living chosen by purposeless people or one which merely adapts to existing personal circumstances which should be changed for the better. Too often, the agreed upon lifestyle (including home environment, work situation, relationships and choices of leisure activities) reflects only survival and neurotic dependency needs instead of providing opportunities for learning and growth. The result is that such a lifestyle reinforces conditions which are already restrictive and devoid of any evidence of spiritual aspirations.

No one can be truly happy unless the soul's innate urge for transcendent experiences is satisfied. As spiritual beings we can never be completely satisfied with marginal function and partial understanding; because at the level of being, we know that the human condition is not our permanent one.

A useful first step is to examine present circumstances, decide on useful approaches, *write a plan of action*, and *immediately initiate positive programs*. Once realistic choices have been made an obvious reorganization of internal resources takes place. Attitude adjustments precede changes in behavior because actions always flow from our mental states and states of consciousness. An initial adjustment to make is that of renouncing (releasing, letting go of) attitudes and their corresponding behaviors which are contrary to avowed purposes. We cannot remain as we are, in attitude, habitual states of consciousness, and behavior, and at the same time expect desired changes.

Immediately eliminate as much confusion—mental, emotional and environmental—from your life as you can. Arrange conditions so they are entirely supportive of learning, constructive experiences, and spiritual growth. Plan and act for the actualization of spiritual awareness, mental peace, emotional maturity, physical wellness, supportive relationships, creative expression, and the fulfillment of soul destiny. Do not settle for anything less than the highest and best of which you are capable of expressing.

In the last section of this book several pages are

How to Experience Spiritual Growth

provided to encourage you to implement your intentional choices to experience inner peace, spiritual growth, and the fulfillment of life's purposes. I encourage you to complete the reading of the preliminary chapters, then use the planning program to actualize your aspirations. Use the forms provided and write your hopes and dreams. To do this, arrange for privacy, in a quiet place where you will not be disturbed. Be still for a few minutes. Let your mind and soul be open to all things possible. Then write as you feel inclined. (Use a separate sheet of paper or a notebook for this purpose, if you prefer.)

This can be an important process in opening your consciousness to the Infinite and to the awakening of your creative capacities. As you write, feel yourself to be attuned with the Power that nourishes the universe, including you. This simple action of writing your hopes and dreams, for yourself and others, is a positive, creative, causative, decision-making choice that will begin processes of change and transformation at deeper levels of your being, mind and body. And since you cannot think a thought or have a feeling which does not in some way influence the universe, changes will also begin to take place in your personal world, in your relationships and environmental circumstances. More, by doing this you will be inviting into your life the beneficial influences of creative forces present in the universe, which will assist you toward the fulfillment of your worthy hopes and dreams. When you include others in your possibility-thinking program, you bless their lives. You will begin to see them differently, relate to them differently, and release from your own mind limiting beliefs and opinions about them.

The Spiritual Basis of Inner Peace

The lasting personal peace every dissatisfied person yearns for can only be experienced as the result of inner realization, which directly results in spontaneous understanding and permanent fulfillment. All other attempts to know peace, while perhaps able to confer a degree of relief from discontent, are but temporary and superficial exercises which may somewhat pacify the mind and create an illusion of soul peace.

To experience the blessedness of peace of soul we have no other choice than to come to terms with the fact that we are spiritual beings living in a constantly changing world-event and that even our mental and emotional states, which are also constantly undergoing transformation, cannot provide the enduring basis for everlasting soul contentment and security. This is why all attempts to create and maintain personal peace, and peace among groups and nations, if directed to surface matters only, are never entirely successful. While there are many things we can do to provide for ourselves circumstances which allow us relative comfort and degrees of freedom from stress, so that we can more easily cultivate our higher qualities and grow in the direction of spiritual maturity, it should be understood that comfortable outer circumstances and functional, conditioned states of consciousness are but supports. They, too, as are all relative circumstances, are subject to change. There is no lasting promise of predictable security in the realm of externals (and our inner world of mental processes is external to soul awareness) until we are anchored in conscious realization of our nature as being, and in our relationship with God.

It is certainly advisable to arrange outer conditions so

that the necessities of life are easily provided, resources are available, and supportive relationships are nurtured and maintained. To state that there is no lasting security possible in this world is not a negative assertion—it is merely a truthful determination of the facts which should be confronted and understood. The field of Nature, the universe with its billions of galaxies and their billions of suns, and its gross, subtle, and fine levels of operation, is evolving; therefore constantly changing. Conditions on Planet Earth, as well as political and social circumstances, are constantly changing. Even we are changing. We may even say, "I am not the same person I was yesterday—or last week, last month, or ten or more years ago." We recognize that our thoughts, feelings, moods and desires constantly change. All changes occur on the surface and everything "this side" of the unmanifested field of consciousness is surface (external or outward) compared to the inner field of consciousness which is the only constant. (Likewise, the only changeless aspect of us, is our beingness, our soul nature.)

Because we experience the fact of forever-change in our lives we may sometimes experience a mood of mild disappointment, of being let down or of having been deceived. We thought the world was real (permanent) and that we could be secure in it, only to discover that the things of the world, including conditions and relationships which seem to be meaningful, cannot be depended upon. Circumstances change, what outwardly is becomes "what was," and if we are not intent upon the path of continued discovery the facts of life may cause us distress. Even our most perfectly contrived lifestyle will, sooner or later, compelled by the inexorable flow of evolutionary forces, be transcended as higher stages of spiritual growth are experienced.

But we do not have to physically withdraw from the world to have understanding and to be grounded in peace of soul. We only have to "die to the world" by relinquishing our attachments and dependencies. Since we are in the world we obviously have a karmic reason (our present relationships reflect our states of consciousness and mental-emotional states) or a destined (predetermined) purpose, or both. Thus, we have unfinished business here and will have to learn to do the best we can to increase in understanding, to continue to grow psychologically and spiritually, and to find out how to serve. The key to inner peace and personal freedom, in this or any realm, is to be "in the world but not of it"; to relate to circumstances from higher understanding and with appropriate involvement and response. We have but to learn to see clearly, without illusions (without making errors in judgment), while functioning from soul awareness instead of from conditioned mental states and changing moods. To the degree that we do this (and we can) we find that we are able to enjoy life without grasping at it or rejecting it, and that we can be unwaveringly settled in the blessedness of soul peace.

Ignorance, lack of knowledge, can only be a temporary excuse for making mistakes and for being unfulfilled. Lack of knowledge is at the root of a host of human failings and miseries—emotional immaturity, self-defeating behavior, poverty, most illnesses, loneliness, and all the troubles a human being is subject to while in the conditioned state. But lack of knowledge can be corrected if one is not mentally deficient or lazy. When we are under the spell of illusions we perform accordingly, and often justify our behavior. "I'm only human," we may assert. "I had a painful childhood and never knew what it was to be loved," we may pout. You have heard, as have I, the various self-justifying and self-defensive refrains based on lack of understanding, prompted by an unwillingness to learn, or lack of courage to confront the challenge of personal growth.

We may even become somewhat uncomfortable in our not-really-fulfilling-but-acceptable circumstances and resist useful change because of fear of the unknown. There are millions of people, affluent and poor, healthy and sick, educated and illiterate, almost-wise and ignorant, who have settled for life as it presently is for them because they have found their niche, their place or level of functional expression which provides for them a degree of comfort or personal satisfaction.

There are many people who are self-righteous in their poverty, who only feel special when they are sick, who accept dysfunctional conditions as normal, and who are dogmatic in their efforts to preserve and even promote their abysmal state of ignorance. And even many reasonably intelligent and functional people are attached to their conditioned-condition and resent any invitation to awaken to a more expanded state of consciousness. They may fear losing what they have attained or acquired, not knowing that increased awareness can only contribute to a greater measure of knowledge and function.

It would be an interesting experiment to talk with a number of dysfunctional people and ask a few direct questions, such as: would they like to be more knowledgeable than they presently are, would they like to be more prosperous, would they like to be emotionally mature, would they like to be physically healthy, would they like to live without restrictions, would they like to be able to love and be loved, and would they like to be spiritually enlightened? I wonder how many would respond affirmatively?

You may ask these questions of yourself. I recommend that you do. What are your responses? And what are you choosing to do about possibilities?

I invite you to accept the fact that you can be spiritually aware, you can be mentally healthy and emotionally well, you can be physically healthy, you can be creatively functional, you can fulfill your worthy purposes in life and you can experience redeeming grace. In extending this invitation I am but expressing what knowledgeable men and women, past and present, have said based on their personal experience. This "good news" should be welcomed. It should result in a stirring of soul forces and cause visions of all possibilities to surface in the mind's eye.

In the New Testament account (*The Gospel According to Saint John* 14:8) the disciple Philip said to Jesus, "Lord, show us the Father (God), and it will satisfy us." Many of us might sincerely ask such a question but not be able to confront the obvious changes which might occur in our lives were the processes of transformation necessary to experience higher realization to occur. A shift of consciousness from what is normal for even a highly actualized person, to God consciousness, would be more awesomely revealing than would a shift of consciousness from a primitive human state to the highest possible state of self-consciousness. An adjustment in consciousness from self-consciousness to superconsciousness, then to cosmic consciousness and God consciousness, is possible. But for many people in today's world, to even extend themselves sufficiently to improve present circumstances, is an effort they find too challenging.

We may think we want to improve—but do we? If we really wanted to, we would, for sincere desire reinforced by intention and faith is the primary causative factor in producing results. If we sincerely want to do something, knowledge of how to proceed is not always the first essential, although it is useful. What is needed is the desire, for desire will result in actions (and inner unfoldment) which enable us to acquire knowledge, as well as put into motion the creative forces to fulfill itself. More important than passionate exercise of will, is focused attention which enables us to be in harmony with evolutionary forces which are innately inclined to fulfill purposes when an avenue for their expression is provided. Purposeful desire, along with faith in the creative process, are the principles with which to cooperate in order to experience whatever possible condition or circumstance is desired—including inner peace, spiritual growth and the fulfillment of life's purposes.

Living Can be Natural,
Spontaneous and Enjoyable

To live naturally is to live in harmony with the laws and principles by which Nature operates. Enlightened religious teachers, educated philosophers and people in general with a reasonable degree of intelligence, understand the practical value of living like this. Many scriptures refer to the process as "the way of righteousness," the way of living in harmony with the supportive influences of Nature. If we live this way even without consciously endeavoring to grow spiritually, we will, because the insistent process of evolution will contribute to our growth and maturity. Further, if we live this way and consciously enter into processes which can enhance awareness and improve function, we will experience an acceleration of spiritual growth which will result in progressive unfoldment, complete emotional maturity and illumination of consciousness.

The laws of natural selection are operative in Nature. Living things (including us) which adapt to Nature's conditions and fulfill their purposes, thrive and flourish. Living things (including us) which do not learn to adapt, or choose not to, do not thrive and flourish. For a reasonably intelligent person it is easier to be happy and successful than it is to be unhappy and a failure in life. Why is it, then, that only a small percentage of the human race is self-responsible and successful? To be sure, there are some people who at the moment are just not conscious enough to know any better than to live in their restricted circumstances. But for most reasonably conscious people, the reason they are not doing any better is because they don't want to. They think that life is supposed to be difficult and even painful. Or if they occasionally dream of possibilities, they don't do anything to help themselves because they have settled for conformity, for being like their friends and companions, for being like everyone else they know.

Life can be painful but it does not have to be forever painful. It is painful for the persons ignorant of possibilities and for persons who know of possibilities but who cannot or will not do anything to help themselves learn and grow. Many people are under the illusion that spiritual growth is difficult, that becoming mature is difficult, that having the necessities of life and being able to actualize worthy purposes is difficult. This may be due to faulty education, lack of self-esteem, resistance to learning how to perform better, or neurosis. And neurotic behavior, in most instances, is chosen behavior.

Remember, *our lifestyle should support our aspirations.* If we are attracted to the ideal of being open to life and to experiencing expanded states of consciousness, and their corresponding benefits, but persist in routines and behaviors which are inconsistent with the goals we envision, conflict will result, along with incomplete outcomes. While it is true that our spiritual practices will contribute to beneficial changes in mental attitude and behavior, it is well to also support our aspirations by consciously choosing a lifestyle that is conducive to harmony, health and growth. This will include the choices we make in the relationships we choose to maintain and nurture, what we eat, the intentional service we render to individuals and society, the work that we do, how we use our recreational time, and everything else we do with purpose.

Study for the purpose of learning and self-improvement should be of two kinds. We should be informed about how to relate to our world and function in it. This is the practical aspect of our education which enables us to appreciate life and get along in the world. Of equal importance is metaphysical study—the examination of that which is not always so obvious to surface observation; that which is usually outside the range of ordinary perception and knowledge. Metaphysical studies include the study of

Spiritual Growth Can be Natural

consciousness, God, the soul, and the origins and operations of the universe which can only be known subjectively—the knowledge of which enables us to comprehend the true nature of life.

I recommend a practical approach to metaphysical studies, not an involvement in pseudo-metaphysical theories and practices which will only result in distractions from the major purpose of learning higher principles and their applications.

Learning and growing is not always easy. It is sometimes challenging, but it can be spontaneous and joyous when we begin to experience results, when we willingly enter into the learning and growing process and know it for the great adventure it is. We were introduced into this world to unfold our inborn potential. Once we accept this, surrender to the processes necessary for our growth and learn to let the universe nurture us, we will experience an increasing unfoldment of our capacities as we rapidly awaken to complete understanding.

Psychological and Spiritual Growth Can be Natural, Spontaneous and Enjoyable

Spiritual practices should include self-training in maintaining our understanding that we are spiritual beings already grounded in God, that every person is in reality a divine being, that Nature is a manifestation of divine energy, and that all creatures are units of consciousness involved in their specialized functions. Also included should be any other practice supportive of our desire to experience progressive psychological growth and spiritual unfoldment. These practices may include interludes of honest self-evaluation, affirmative speech and behavior, surrendered prayer, and meditation.

Self-examination affords us the opportunity to remain self-honest and on purpose in life. It affords us the opportunity to come to terms with memories, attitudes, beliefs, purposes and behaviors. Ideally, this should be done while maintaining an objective attitude, fully aware that our spiritual reality is our permanent identity and that when engaged in self-examination we are but learning to better understand our deeper motivations as well as the existence of any inner restricting influences which need to be released. A helpful process is to avoid identifying with memories which cause painful emotional reactions. Instead, recognize them as impressions recorded in the subconscious level of the mind, understand the supporting circumstances, forgive if necessary, and release any suppressed trauma. In this way diminish and eliminate their influences. Self-examination usually should not be done when emotionally depressed, over-tired, or under the influence of stress. At such times it may be difficult to confront and process what is being examined. Maintain a confident and capable attitude. Avoid attitudes of dependency or helplessness.

Except in unusual circumstances a reasonably functional person will not have to seek out the regular emotional support of others who have similar personal challenges or arrange for private therapy. In obvious instances of need for assistance, pastoral or psychological (or both) counseling and help may be helpful, after first doing some research to be certain that the person whose assistance is invited is qualified to meet one's needs; that is, that he or she is educated, psychologically mature and spiritually orientated.

To enter into long-term relationships with persons who gather on a regular schedule for the purpose of supporting each other because of having common needs, is not recommended for one who is committed to a self-actualization program and desires real psychological and spiritual growth. Support groups can be helpful, but they can also become convenient gatherings which prolong the problem of dependency. Support groups should be just

Spiritual Growth Can be Natural

that: loving environments of support and encouragement which eventually result in their transient members being able to do without them. Core members of such a group should be mature enough to facilitate this process.

Prayer is the process of communing with God, by verbal or mental conversation or by quietly resting and being open to an awareness of the presence and reality of God. No great skill is required in the prayer process. The less complicated it is, the more satisfying will be the response. A most useful approach is to simply sit still and talk with God. An honest talk with God is good therapy. Just talk with God until talking ceases, then be still and commune with God in the deep silence. In this way prayer leads naturally to contemplative meditation.

Meditation is a relaxed, conscious (not passive) process of sitting, with attention flowing to the field of pure consciousness. This field is all pervasive and is the underlying strata of consciousness which supports objective reality. Therefore, when feelings and thought processes become refined to the extent that their influences are minimal, the meditator easily experiences his own soul nature as pure being as well as the unbounded field of pure consciousness of which his consciousness is a specialized unit. Regular episodes of superconscious meditation provide deep rest for mind and body, reduction of stress in the nervous system and allows the meditator to actually experience his existence as being independent of mental operations and bodily functions*.

Psychological and spiritual growth can be natural, spontaneous and enjoyable because progressive growth removes confusion, mental dullness, and emotional unrest. Relieved of these disturbing influences, one becomes happier, more optimistic, purposeful and enthusiastic. One's appreciation for living is enhanced and aspirations to actualize higher purposes become more pronounced. Self-esteem improves and a heightened moral sense unfolds. One naturally "becomes a better person" and is

---

* See the third section of this book for precise meditation instruction.

inclined to cultivate the virtues and progress to increased understanding and function. Happiness becomes more pronounced and a cheerful demeanor, characterized by willingness to communicate and enjoy life, results in an expansion of consciousness.

As we become more aware and functional, we become more spontaneous, instinctively and intuitively able to make right choices, and accomplish purposes with less effort without having to struggle with decision-making processes. We can even learn to appreciate occasions of necessary challenge (due to having to rid ourselves of nonuseful inner conditions as well as having to learn how to accomplish purposes) because of knowing that the final result will be the permanent removal of delusion, illusion and all circumstances which formerly interfered with conscious living. It is not always pleasant to come to terms with transitional events (which we might like to have persist) or our own obvious short-comings. It is not always easy to forgive ourselves, and others, and to give up what is no longer useful in favor of that which is more useful.

Until a reasonable degree of psychological and spiritual growth unfolds, some distress will usually be experienced. This comes with the conditioned-condition and cannot usually be avoided, though it can be minimized as understanding improves and emotional maturity becomes more pronounced. As a result, we develop character, become more philosophical, and possessed of a more profound and satisfying degree of understanding. We become more sage-like.

How to Have the Courage to Live and be Fulfilled

While attending a New Thought conference in a western U.S. city, I was asked to present a five-minute inspirational talk as a segment of the evening program. Before

How to Have the Courage to Live

going from my hotel room to the auditorium, I sat quietly to meditate, then opened my mind to a flow of creative ideas. My question, to myself, was, "What can I say in five minutes that will be meaningful and helpful to each of the hundreds of persons present?" What came to mind was, "What almost every person needs to know, is how to have the courage to live and be fulfilled." So that message was the one I shared with the people that night.

Fear, uncertainty, lack of self-confidence—these feelings are commonly admitted by most people at one time or another. Even devotees on a spiritual path are not exempt from such feelings. Courage is always needed if we are to confront ourselves and get on with the practical business of ordering our lives and actualizing our abilities in order to manifest our worthy hopes and dreams. To be fearless, remember the truth of your being—you are made in the image and likeness of God and all of the attributes and capacities of God are within you. Remember, also, that with God, all things possible can be actualized. They can manifest in fact. To eliminate uncertainty, see to your complete education so that you are well informed, then proceed with faith.

We may say that we have confidence in God, but do we have confidence in ourselves? Are we confident of our own abilities, our own capacities, our own worthiness? We have inborn abilities which only need to be nurtured and correctly used. We have almost limitless capacities which only need to be unfolded. We are certainly worthy of fulfillment because this is what we came into this world to experience.

The most practical way to cultivate confidence and courage is to fully commit to a planned program of growth-enhancing procedures; that is, to be immediately involved, and persist with dedication, in disciplined routines and practices which will definitely result in the unfoldment of desired outcomes. In this way you will learn-by-doing and acquire experience which will confirm the usefulness of your actions.

Allow no space in your consciousness for guilt or

remorse because of "what might have been" had you only performed better prior to the present moment. Just begin and everything will certainly improve from this moment forward. If necessary, begin anew as often as necessary until your soul-inspired motivational drives keep you effortlessly on course. As the days, weeks, and months unfold you will become a different person (a more actualized personality) even while learning to remain anchored in soul consciousness and God awareness. The doors of heaven (the consciousness of your true nature and the realization of fulfillment) will open without fail.

We are not asked to do the impossible, we are only invited to do our best. As we do our human and divine best, the natural result is spiritual growth and progressive unfoldment of creative abilities. Material fulfillment is included in spiritual fulfillment because there are no spaces between levels of manifest consciousness. A saint once said to a disciple, "Few mortals know that the kingdom of heaven extends fully to this Earth plane."

The writing and speaking aloud of specific affirmations, which clearly define and declare our inner convictions and intentions is a powerful result-producing process. The correct use of affirmations is not a simplistic procedure. I know, some people do use affirmations as a way to pacify the mind and provide emotional comfort, while not understanding the potency of affirmations when correctly used. However, I recommend that you train yourself to write and speak affirmations with conscious intention and inner realization, with results following.

The purpose of using affirmations is not that of further conditioning the mind or to lull consciousness into a passive state. Affirmations, rightly used, help us order our thoughts, eliminate negative feelings, focus on essentials and actually *consciously realize* the truth of that which is affirmed. Some affirmations follow. If you want to, you may stand in front of a mirror and look yourself in the eye as you affirm these positive statements and feel their life-changing influences.

FOR SPIRITUAL GROWTH

Because I am an individualized unit of consciousness I am literally made in the image and likeness of God. I rejoice in this understanding. I easily and spontaneously do whatever is helpful to contribute to my further awakening and full God-realization. At the deepest level of my being I am now grounded in the Infinite. I am conscious, happy, serene, peaceful and complete.

FOR IMPROVED MENTAL CREATIVITY

My mind is a portion of Cosmic Mind, the Mind of God. I spontaneously use my mental faculties in cooperation with God's will. My thoughts are naturally well-ordered, decisions are easily made, my mental attitude is always positive, and I intuitively use my creative abilities to assist desirable and worthy outcomes.

FOR EMOTIONAL STABILITY

Because I am grounded in the Infinite I am always calm and centered. I enjoy life and relate to others and my world easily and appropriately. I handle memories of the past, and present circumstances, with objectivity and grace. I am established in inner peace. I am happy, I am thankful.

FOR PHYSICAL HEALTH AND VITALITY

My body is the temple of the Holy Spirit. I do all useful and natural things to allow God to be glorified through my body temple. While attending to practical routines and procedures, I remain open to the activity of the all-radiant nourishing influences of Cosmic Life Force which sustains and nourishes me and all beings.

FOR SUPPORTIVE RELATIONSHIPS

I see the world and all things in it as manifestations of God's creative energy. I see all people as divine beings and relate to them with love and respect. I accept love and supportive relationships easily and joyfully while extending myself to share love and support to others and my world. God is my constant companion and never-failing True Friend. I am open to God as all nourishing expressions of life.

FOR SUCCESS IN WORTHY VENTURES
I am committed to doing God's will. I am committed to serving the cause of evolution. I am committed to the way of righteousness. Everything I do is done in the understanding that I am an individualized expression of God and that my purpose in this world is to allow God's intentions to be expressed through and around me.

Also, use affirmations in a contemplative way. Sit quietly and enter into a meditative mood. Speak the affirmation aloud, with feeling and conviction, several times. Continue to speak the affirmation aloud and with successive repetitions gradually speak progressively softer, from normal speaking to quiet speaking, to whispered speaking, then to mental speaking, and finally to thoughtless *acceptance, feeling,* and *realization* of the essence of the affirmation. Rest in this realization for as long as comfortable to allow it to become permanent in your consciousness.

Thereafter, act in accordance with your new understanding and your new awareness of yourself in relationship to your world. This is the key—to become the embodiment of that which is affirmed*.

Why All Human Problems Must (and do) Have a Spiritual Solution

Any solution to a human problem, that does not have a basis of spiritual awareness and influence, is but a temporary adjustment of circumstances because it is without

---

*After writing the above affirmations I did what I recommend to you. I stood before a mirror and experienced them with conviction, feeling, and realization. I have taken them into my consciousness. They are therefore "spiritualized" and impregnated with superconscious influence, and their usefulness thereby enhanced.

a permanent foundation. Problems of any kind have causes at deeper levels which create and support disharmony. These deeper causes must be removed if problems are to be completely resolved, without their contributing causes resulting in future problems of a similar nature.

For instance, disease symptoms may be repressed by medication or other procedures, but total health cannot be said to exist so long as deep-seated contributing causes remain at subtle levels, or in a dormant condition. Again, an outer semblance of harmony may be established in a human relationship because of participants agreeing to observe common courtesies and communication modes which are socially appropriate, but if underlying resentments or other conflicts are merely repressed, difficulties in relationships may manifest at any moment when circumstances trigger a reaction. As another example, a business may be flourishing so far as procedures flowing smoothly and services being rendered, but if the cash reserve is low and plans for growth and expanded service are not going forward, it may be on an unstable basis. Therefore, surface appearances can sometimes be illusory. Restoring a sick person to a condition of reasonable health, maintaining appropriate social interactions, and experiencing a flow of productivity in a business enterprise are useful, but all outer expressions of life should be realistically grounded in something more permanent than a temporary holding pattern. (Airplane pilots are sometimes requested by the control tower operator to fly in a circle near the destination airport, to await further instructions for landing. They are still functional and there may be no apparent operational problems, but their flight is not completed until they land the airplane. Similarly, a person may be functional in his lifestyle, with no apparent problems being visible, but not be completely healthy or fulfilled because his life is not yet grounded in the Infinite.)

The wellness I am emphasizing is *total wellness*—not partial or temporary wellness, but wellness that remains as a reflection of soul realization. I would recommend that the reader not be satisfied with partial spiritual awareness, partial mental efficiency, partial emotional maturity, partial physical health, partially acceptable human relationships, or partial fulfillment of purposes. Many people do settle for less than what is possible. They try to cover up their discontent by saying, "Regardless of circumstances which are not satisfying, my faith in God is a great comfort to me," or, "At least I'm smarter than most people I know," "I have some problems but I'll get by," and "I'm not doing too badly; after all, a person can't have everything."

True, in order to get along with others we often make trade-offs and adjustments, especially for the purpose of maintaining a degree of social harmony, but if we do we should at least be conscious of why we do it and be comfortable with our choices. If we are not comfortable with our choices we will likely be frustrated, even resentful. Emotional unrest may then contribute to further problems, such as outbursts of temper, mood swings and depression, addictive behavior of various kinds, accidents, a tendency to fall back into destructive habit patterns, and even physical complaints or serious illness.

Many people who have addictive personalities (although the description is suspect because people often manifest addictive behaviors without having obvious characteristics of neurosis) will admit to feeling "empty inside," with little sense of awareness of God or only a vague idea of purpose for their lives. This feeling of isolation, of being separated from God, is a perfect description of hell on Earth. It therefore follows that a dependent person needs to grow spiritually by admitting to the necessity of it and turning to the Higher Power, to God, for assistance. We may hear someone say, "My life is working. I have all I need. I certainly don't need religion, or God!" When we hear this kind of talk, we are hearing foolishness. Everyone may not need to be involved with a formal religious tradition, but everyone needs an understanding of, and relationship with, God.

There is not one thing we do that is isolated from the rest of our behavior and that does not, to some degree, influence our lifestyle. Sly, deceptive behavior in one area of our lives may well manifest in another, if not obviously, then at deeper levels where psychological conflicts impair our judgment and confuse our emotions. Anything we do that is contrary to the highest ideals we have for ourselves (the things we do that we know are not right for us) can cause conflict, guilt, prevent open communication with others, and interfere with our growth and progress. The most damaging effects are upon ourselves because inner conflict interferes with interactions occurring between unconscious, subconscious and conscious levels of the mind. Every unenlightened person has areas of the mind which are occluded; that is, closed off or inaccessible. Sometimes unconscious influences emerge during dreams, when we are more subconscious than conscious. When unconscious drives break through during our waking states we may experience hallucinations. This can occur when we are very tired, when deprived of sleep, or when mental processes are so disordered that we are "out of touch with reality." An obvious manifestation of mental disorder is schizophrenia, a separating of personality components to the extent that one behaves unreasonably and manifests a variety of personalities and behaviors. When conflict between unconscious and conscious levels of mind is dramatic we say a person is insane, incapable of making rational judgments and irresponsible outside the range of what is considered normal.

Many normal people in society are irrational and irresponsible in comparison with functional, actualized people, and most functional and actualized human beings still have progress ahead of them before awakening to higher states of consciousness.

It is well for us to be entirely self-honest and as self-responsible and competent as we can be, in order to create as healthy an inner environment as possible for continued spiritual growth. Partial measures are for those lacking knowledge and courage, half-way measures are for the uncommitted, one-hundred percent focus is for those who have a vision of ultimate possibilities and who are resolved to attain the spiritual heights. I hope you are among the increasing numbers of the latter category.

Good intentions are not always sufficient to enable us to accomplish our worthy purposes. Witness how many people you have heard say, when falling short or failing, "I meant well." Good intentions are admirable, but more useful are constructive actions; not only outer actions when needed, but inner actions, inner adjustments of attitude and states of consciousness. While outer evidence of progress is encouraging and can boost our self-confidence, the real power is inside at deeper levels of being where we are grounded in the Infinite. The ocean wave has behind it the power of the ocean, and we have behind us the power of God. When grounded in God we are invincible because the forces of Nature cooperate with us.

No matter the appearance of an external problem, whether it appears to us to be small or large, spiritual understanding and the nourishing influence of grace is more than equal to it. Remember, everything in the field of Nature, you and me included, is within the body of God. Any belief as to the impossibility of a problem of any kind being solved, is our own. Sometimes we may feel despair because circumstances seem difficult to change, or because we are having trouble changing as we would like to change.

If we are living a natural, balanced life and unfoldments are progressive and orderly, we can go with the flow. We are surely on the upward path and evolutionary forces are presently influential to the extent that the fulfillment of soul destiny is assured. On the other hand, if we are not living a natural, balanced life and problems not only persist but increase, we are in need of inner transformation which can result in constructive changes.

Some people not only live with their problems, they defend them. A television news program presented a short segment showing a group of extremely obese (life-threateningly overweight) men and women who had formed a support group to rally other obese people to their cause. Their calls to involvement included, "Speak up! Say, 'I like being fat!'" and, "Fat is beautiful!" Others may say, "Junk food doesn't hurt me! A little grease, salt and white sugar never hurt anybody!" or, "I like to drink alcohol, it blocks out the world so I don't have to see it." An increasing number of people who have succeeded in controlling some of their more life-threatening addictions have become involved in support groups for the purpose of maintaining function and to help others who need encouragement. Most such groups have a spiritual basis for their programs because experienced members know that God's grace is necessary if permanent, useful change is to be actualized.

A major reason why some people are addicted (attached) to destructive behaviors is because they have no interesting plans for the near or distant future. They have nothing of value to look forward to, no direction or purpose in life. The meaning of life will not be found "out there," the meaning of life is experienced when we live life well; in harmony with Nature's rhythms and purposes. But we may not have this vision of possibilities. We may, instead, be trapped in our little, personal world. A woman may be the "perfect" wife and mother, only to fall apart mentally and emotionally when her mate dies or leaves her, or when the children grow and leave home. A man or woman may enjoy working, yet become aimless and confused after retirement. A person may be rich in all that the world has to offer, yet be spiritually bankrupt. The need to be needed is innate to us. Understood, and intelligently and compassionately expressed, this need to be needed can result in creative involvements with life which can bless us and all whom our lives influence. If not intelligently and compassionately expressed, frustrated urges can cause us emotional pain and complicate our lives, as well as the lives of those with whom we have relationships.

Life does not cease for us when someone we care about withdraws from us or is taken away by circumstances beyond their control, when children grow up, or when we are asked to retire from a job. Life goes on, and there is always an abundance of opportunity for continued growth, for continued giving, when we are open to opportunities and willing to extend ourselves.

We will examine the matter of physical (and other) healing later in this text, along with procedures for implementing the awakening of the healing powers within us. Now, however, I am planting seeds of faith in your mind by informing you of the *indisputable* ("absolute and incontrovertible") truth that there can be no lasting solutions to problems of any kind without spiritual understanding and influence.

*Prospering Can be Natural,
Enjoyable and Spontaneous*

To *prosper* is "to thrive, to flourish, to be successful." My guru Paramahansa Yogananda used to say, "He is wisest who seeks God. He is the most successful who realizes God." Living things, when not restricted, naturally thrive and flourish, they naturally fulfill life's purposes. We should thrive, flourish and fulfill life's purposes just as naturally. If we are not living like this it must be because of restrictions of one kind or another. These restrictions can be discovered, and eliminated.

Whenever we hear ourselves justifying limitation, we know we have a problem. Remember, the primary problem is lack of understanding and the major restrictions are self-centeredness and laziness. If we are reasonably intelligent and are willing to learn how to function, we can become knowledgeable, extend our awareness beyond the boundaries of egoism and learn by doing. We can then satisfy our legitimate needs, grow spiritually and fulfill life's purposes.

Imagine how life will be for you when you are living without restrictions because you are knowledgeable, spontaneous and flowing with the currents of life! Can you imagine it? If you have not yet explored the possibilities of imagination (or have, but have been neglecting the practice) learn to do so, for until enlightenment fully unfolds your ability to imagine possibilities is one of the most useful skills you have for intentionally adjusting states of consciousness and influencing circumstances. This side of the field of pure consciousness (as long as we are in relative spheres), the partial dreamlike character of our existence determines that most of our experiences be imaginal: reflections of our states of consciousness and mental states. Controlled imagination, then, is an available mental-spiritual process for being somewhat responsible for our experiences and circumstances. I say *somewhat* because no person can completely determine his life, because providence is also influential and often intervenes to assist us—sometimes, thankfully, in spite of ourselves.

We may be blessed with a healthy physical constitution but experience restrictions in other areas of our lives. We may be subject to mood changes, find it difficult to concentrate, have little or no curiosity about what goes on about us, have difficulties in relationships, or not be happy with our present job situation. We may be reasonably materially successful but be overstressed, have psychological problems, or occasions of physical distress. We may not yet have come to terms with the traumas of childhood or outgrown immature ways of thinking and behavior. But the vision of possibilities I present to you is a life without limiting restrictions—a conscious, healthy, creatively functional, spiritually aware, totally fulfilled life.

Even if our immediate needs are met and our relationships are satisfactory, without psychological and spiritual growth we are not prosperous. We may think that if our material needs are taken care of without too much hardship, and that we "have someone to love, who loves us," we are well off. But this is only the beginning, not the end of our journey. Life should be more than survival and security. Life should be maintenance, a degree of security, and abundant opportunity for continued spiritual growth and expression. With this in mind let's examine practical ways to prosper: naturally, spontaneously and enjoyably.

Again, there are three ways to the accomplishment of any purpose: the *most difficult way*, the *easier way*, and the *easiest way*. Or, the way of *most effort*, the way of *least effort*, and the way of *no effort*.

Even effortless projects, if we are personally involved, will require the expenditure of some personal energy even though the end results are already assured because of imaginal acts and inward realizations. For instance, to attain physical skills and contribute to body function, even if one has a "health consciousness" one will have to maintain a schedule of activity and rest, attend to nutritional needs, and to other matters relative to the process. If one has a "success consciousness" and is personally involved with projects, a certain amount of time and energy will have to be given to relationships and duties. To earn a college degree, attain proficiency in any practice, or to demonstrate talents, one will have to be involved personally as part of the unfoldment of the imaginal process. However, there are many things that can be accomplished without our personal involvement, beyond that of exercising gentle intention and perhaps using imagination creatively.

The *most difficult way* to accomplish purposes, the way of *most effort* and the way which is limited by personal time and available energy, is the way of working at surface levels. At this level of operation one may endeavor to ensure physical health by attending to commonly known procedures while not being aware of the usefulness of cultivating a "health consciousness" or the role that imagination and visualization can play in the process. One may attempt to attain psychological health by making minor adjustments in attitude and by processing only surface problem-causing conflicts and behaviors, without getting to deeper causes and eliminating them. One may attempt to have comfortable social relationships by learning the rules of social interaction, without really trying to learn how to love and be loved, how to care about others and accept caring from them. One may work hard, using time and energy for an agreed upon wage but seldom get beyond

Prospering Can be Natural

the level of being reasonably financially secure. One may worship in a ritualistic way and observe the letter of the law of religious teachings, but not have an inner comprehension of the nature of Higher Reality or even be completely clear about why he does what he does. These are outer ways, the ways of most effort and the least fulfilling ways to proceed. They are, however, superior to the sometimes alternative of withdrawing into hopeless despair or escaping into destructive, addictive behaviors.

The *easier way*, the way of *least effort*, is the way of possibility-thinking, conscious decision making, rational planning, the creative exercise of imagination, and enthusiastic participation. This requires the use of our executive abilities. It requires a willingness to learn, to grow psychologically and spiritually, to be courageous and imbued with faith, and to learn how to be open to the benevolent Power that sustains the universe. With this approach to achieving goals and accomplishing purposes, spiritual growth is spontaneous because the process contributes to the expansion of our consciousness and demands that we learn to adapt to inner changes and outer transitional circumstances. We learn how to better use our time and resources by focusing on productive means and eliminating nonproductive ones. More, because of our expanded metaphysical understanding, we learn how to correctly use mental and spiritual laws of causation and how to be open to the nurturing influences of cosmic forces circulating throughout the field of Nature. We become increasingly aware (and knowledgeable because of experience) that through our minds we have direct access to Universal Mind and that it is responsive to our needs and desires. Further, we learn that the divine intelligence increasingly directs our thought processes, actions, and sequences of outer events. We may begin by thinking that we are in charge of our lives, only to discover, as we proceed, that a Higher Power is becoming more obviously expressive through us.

The *easiest way*, the way of *no effort*, is referred to in religious literature as the way of grace. Thankfully, grace is operative in our lives even when we are not conscious of it or able to recognize its actions. It is that which takes care of us and contributes to our growth and welfare when we help ourselves—and even when we do almost everything wrong. This is why it is called the gift of God. Its innate characteristic, expressing as the impulse of evolution, is to ensure transformation, growth, and the completion of worthy purposes.

We can learn to be open to grace and experience its redemptive influence in our lives. We do this by learning to rest in the awareness of being, either during meditation or at other times when we choose to be inwardly centered and reminded of our relationship with God. When we rest at this level of awareness, whatever we need is provided us by the universe. Whatever we want to see unfold, if it is in harmony with Nature's laws, will unfold effortlessly. At this level of awareness, taking no anxious thought about the sequence of processes which may be required to fulfill dreams and complete projects, we have but to inwardly accept desired outcomes and our acceptance will attract favorable circumstances into our lives—ideal relationships, ideal opportunities, ideal happenings, ideal everything! What many do not know is that what is needed by them is already available for the accepting. One saint said, "Even if what you need (or want) is not presently in manifestation, the universe will manifest it for you if you need it or want it." Out of formless consciousness, all forms emerge into manifestation. Out of chaos, harmony can unfold. Darkness can be removed by light. Ignorance can be replaced by wisdom. Sorrow can be dispelled by joy. Sickness, poverty, and any and all discordant conditions can be eliminated by grace. The shadows of this world can be manipulated by imaginal acts and regulated by divine insistence.

The first way, the way of most effort, *is to work at the level of physical causation; regulating circumstances by material influence.* The second way, the way of less effort, *is to function from the level of mental and imaginal causation.* The third way, the way of no effort, *is to rest in pure consciousness and let grace abound,* or *to rest in pure consciousness and provide an avenue through which grace can be directed by maintaining a gentle intention for desired unfoldments.*

Until we are settled in selflessness, even while working from the level of least effort there can be some egocentric influences present. We may mistakenly assume that now that we know the metaphysical way of causing effects we can assert ourselves, dominate others and the environment, and be the complete master of our destiny. Ego-motivated attainment will in all likelihood turn to ashes and leave a bitter taste. Just the same, it is by doing that we learn. If mistakes in judgment are made, they can be corrected. If we create problems for ourselves, we can solve them by learning to use our creative abilities correctly. Before embarking upon any project it is best to pray, meditate, and be open to guidance. It is best to think of end results and whether or not they will be a blessing for everyone involved, as well as nurturing to Planet Earth. Unfoldments and ends must be entirely benevolent and constructive.

Some people on the spiritual path are reluctant to use their decision-making and imaginal abilities for fear of making mistakes. They may sincerely feel that they do not want to be willful. We are supposed to use our God-endowed abilities for righteous purposes. We are supposed to help ourselves. Even when grace is operative in our lives, there will be occasions when we will have to keep our appointments, attend to duties, and use our intelligence to make right choices.

God's grace can put food on the table and pay the rent. Imagination can also facilitate these processes. But it is also a good idea to know how to do practical things to provide for ourselves. Imagination can awaken healing forces in the body, but it may be well for the patient to also attend to other matters which have a bearing on the healing process, such as: clearing mental and emotional conflicts and cooperating with therapeutic procedures which can bring the body into alignment with Nature's healing forces. The best approach is to function from the level of understanding which enables us to accomplish our purposes in the most efficient manner, while being open to continued spiritual growth and the supportive currents of life from inner levels. At all levels of function (and increasingly important as we become competent at more subtle levels) ethical and moral behavior is essential. Absolute harmlessness, absolute honesty, and absolute purity of motive are the requirements. No harm will come to a person who is grounded in righteousness and no harm will result from his actions.

To prosper in all ways requires an attunement, and open relationship, with life processes. Self-centeredness is the cause of isolation, fear, greed, meanness, and all of the perverted characteristics and behaviors dramatized by human beings. Even when we are somewhat open, if we are still emotionally immature we will tend to behave inappropriately. How we use our abilities and resources and how we relate to others reveals our degree of emotional maturity. We see commercial advertisements offering us the best in creature comforts. We are bombarded with suggestions to grab all we can because life only goes around once and we'd better get our share before we die, or before someone else gets it first. We may even chuckle when a wealthy business man is quoted in the press as saying, "My philosophy is that the person who dies with the most toys, wins." If we relate to that statement, if we believe it, we are in spiritual trouble.

And, yet, in this or any world we will still have to relate to our environment. We will still have to be self-responsible for our actions and experiences. How best to do it? We are in this world for but a relatively brief duration. Death of the body is only a transitional episode for, at transition, we continue to experience life in subtle spheres. The recommended way to relate to the world is to see it for what it is—a play of cosmic forces undergoing transformation. We can then, with practice, learn to live here without grasping at anything and without feeling any aversion to relating to the world or to performing our duties. We can learn to play whatever role may be ours to play, skillfully and while centered in peace of soul. To do this we have to rid ourselves of attitudes and behaviors which are contrary to our major purposes, but this can easily be done.

I was once sharing some of these thoughts during a seminar program and a person said to me, "I didn't come here to hear about how to live in this world. I came here to learn about God." Well, the truth of the matter is, we are here to live in this world in the highest and best way and we can't do it by ignoring the rules of the game. Here and now, *where* and *when* we are in space-time, is the only place and the only interlude in time we have to get clear about who we are and to relate appropriately with the universe and God. Lessons learned *here* and *now* will enable us to function more effectively in future places and other times.

The prosperity idea has been talked about for centuries and most of the sacred books of the world offer advice on how to prosper. Success and achievement books, courses and seminars are increasingly available to the public. Yet the totally prosperous people of the world are a minority group. Only a few, among the many, are really materially prosperous and fewer still are prospering physically, mentally, emotionally, in relationships, and spiritually. Isn't this a strange, even ludicrous, situation? An estimate based on careful research states that if the present population of the planet were reduced to one-thousand persons only 6 people would control all the wealth. Five-hundred would be homeless. Six-hundred would be hungry. Seven-hundred would be illiterate. And how many, do you suppose, would be spiritually enlightened?

Every year I meet thousands of men and women, at lecture events and conferences, and talk personally with hundreds of them. I also know a lot of people who have written self-help books, ministers, and professional helpers of various disciplines. And do you know something?— I have never had anyone tell me, "Roy, I've just got to share something with you. Since I've been studying about these principles and using them, I've gotten completely healthy and I'm truly prosperous." On one level, I understand the human condition. On another level, I sometimes think, to myself, "My God! How can we make these teachings real to people who are sincerely looking for help? How can *I* make them more real to myself so that I can radiate the reality of them?" I do not separate myself from the human family or the myriads of souls working out their salvation (their spiritual freedom) in other times and spaces. I realize that I share the field of Nature with all other beings and I also share their opportunities of growth and personal challenge. But the question persists (perhaps in your mind and heart, also), "When are we going to wake up?"

The subject of money is frequently talked about in some circles; usually most vocally by those who have some and want more, or by those who don't have any, and want some. There are a few people who have a lot and brag about it, some who have a lot and use it wisely, some who are managing quite well, and many who are having difficulties because of a personal lack of available resources.

A young business man of my acquaintance, who is also a lay minister, said to me, "You know, some people have weird ideas about money!" Some people have weird ideas about a lot of things, and money is one thing some people do have unrealistic ideas about.

Money is a convenient medium of exchange. It is not wealth in itself, though it may be a symbol of wealth. It may be evidence of a prosperity consciousness, although there are some miserly people who have either inherited great wealth or who have no problem acquiring it. It is possible to have material security but still feel insecure, unworthy, or even guilty about such good fortune. Occasionally an article will appear in the daily newspaper reporting a big winner in a state lottery. Follow-up reports reveal that some winners welcome their newly found financial freedom and intelligently use their fortune to

Prospering Can be Natural

improve their lives and the lives of others. Some winners just put the money in the bank and continue their routine lifestyle because they are content doing what they have always done. A few winners "go crazy" and waste it all, or become depressed. According to a media report, one person couldn't handle his unexpected good fortune and committed suicide.

How we relate to money may be an indication of how we relate in other areas of our lives. How we handle money certainly indicates how we live our lives. Are we prudent and wise in the use of money, or are we irresponsible and foolish? Do we use it for constructive purposes, or do we use it to manipulate others, or to satisfy our emotional needs? Are we attached to it, or are we afraid of it? Do we label it good or evil? Do we think it right to be prosperous, or do we feel guilty about wanting to be prosperous? What positive ideas do we have about money? What negative ideas to we have about money?

I read a story about a "saintly" man in India who, when a relative placed a coin in his hand while he was asleep, instantly woke up, flung the coin away and displayed a blister on his hand where the coin had touched it. A saint he may have been, but he obviously had an aversion to handling money. (Saints are supposed to see everything as a manifestation of "one thing," everything as consciousness and everything with its own function.)

I have to be informed about many things. I write, publish, travel, lecture, counsel, direct ministry activities, and remain aware of what is happening while planning for near and distant future events. I have never been employed by a secular business and have never had a manager or supervisor to whom I was answerable. Yet, because of what I do I have had to be aware of money and its usefulness. Money, being a unit of exchange, is used to pay the legitimate costs of maintaining and expanding the ministry. But I have never thought of earning money, I am only service-oriented. The more service that is rendered, the better is the money-flow even though the flow is not always directly related to the specific service rendered or the people who are personally served. I have discovered (and am still learning) that to the degree we are open to life, and serving as we are meant to serve, everything else, including money if it is needed, comes into manifestation—often through circumstances and channels which cannot be predicted.

All of my services are given freely. I do not even receive royalty payments for books I write which are published by our publishing firm. When I speak at public meetings or at church gatherings, there is never any admission charge if I have anything to do with the arrangements. At churches a donation is accepted by the sponsoring group and shared with Center for Spiritual Awareness. The donation is not referred to as a "love offering," which seems to me a trite reference to the giving process, sounds like an apology, and hints that meager (deficient in quantity or quality, without fullness or richness) financial participation is encouraged. I know that some people will attend my programs and spend more in the hotel restaurant than they donate for a program of four hours of meditation instruction and practice. They will have to eat again in a few hours, but if they learn to meditate correctly they can know life eternal, but their perception of what is most valuable to them is not always clear. Their behavior is not my problem, for my function is to give. I have noticed that participants who are financially generous are also usually more functional.

A poll taken of a cross section of the general public indicated that giving people are usually happier people. Happy people are more open, more relaxed, more giving, more in tune with life. Unhappy people are not so open, are usually overstressed, tend to be introverted, and are not attuned to life. One way to become happier is to learn to give to life—to receive from the *source* and to give to the *source* by cheerfully participating in life's processes. To be *affluent* means to be "flowing freely." Life can't very well flow through us if we aren't open to it. Life can't very well provide for us if we are not able to relate to its processes.

What if we have nothing to give? Everyone has something to give; if not available money for worthy purposes, then love and caring, goodwill, volunteer services, prayer support, a clear consciousness, and a willing heart. Yes, everyone has something to give and whatever is given should be given freely. The metaphysical key is, when we give in the right spirit and with right understanding, we become increasingly open to the flow which has origins in the field of God, our cosmic Self.

To give in order to receive may be useful in the beginning stages, when we are just learning about the process, because we may then learn about the laws of causation. But a higher way is to give because we have, and we cannot give if we do not have anything to give. So, giving confirms our having. When we understand that we already have an abundance of life within us because we are grounded in the Infinite, we also understand that we are but stewards of the resources available to us and conduits through which inexhaustible resources flow into expression. This is a more expanded understanding of the prosperity process than that of functioning from the level of thinking that we have to bargain with the universe by giving and getting. When we "have it" in our consciousness it will manifest outwardly in whatever form necessary to meet needs, our own or those of others with whom we share our lives.

If we are not used to giving, the best way to begin is to intentionally plan a giving program and follow through with diligence. We can always give spontaneously of our consciousness, our love, and our caring support in whatever way seems most useful. We may not always have too much time to give, and until we are prospering financially we may not always have much money to give. But if we do have a reasonable flow of money, we should give some on a regular schedule to worthwhile endeavors. Many services available to the public are made possible because of the financial contributions of caring people—some hospitals, clinics, research institutes, schools, various community programs, museums, public radio and television broadcasts, churches, and more. It is a matter of record, for instance, that of the average protestant church membership, 15 percent of the membership makes possible the financial support of 80 percent of the budget. Perhaps 20 or 30 percent do the best they can, and the rest give sparingly or only when motivated to do so. We can easily tell what is important to us by how we give of our energy and support. Our lives bear mute witness to our states of consciousness. How we are relating to our world, on all levels and in every aspect, is how we are living our lives.

On Waking Up, Growing Up and Facing Up to Reality

Our entire journey through space-time is a progressive experience in psychological and spiritual growth; a process of waking up, growing to maturity and learning to confront and relate to what is real—the facts of life. Whether the process is enjoyable, or painful, will depend upon the mental attitude we choose from which to view our world. We can choose to cooperate with evolutionary processes and experience the joy of surprising discovery, along with occasional discomfort because of having to adjust to new inner and outer circumstances. We can also choose the painful way, the way of being forced to grow in spite of our reluctance to do so.

Perhaps you can remember your growing experiences as you progressed from early childhood to adolescence, then through your teenage years and emergence into the adult phases of your life. If you made the journey with reasonable success you learned to adapt, explore possibilities, and from time to time leave behind attitudes and behaviors which were no longer useful to the more mature stages of life. It is like this with continued psychological and spiritual growth. If we are to succeed in unfolding our full potential, if we are to succeed in knowing and experiencing all things possible, we have to be willing to discard attitudes and behaviors which are no longer useful to our more expanded world-view and to the fulfillment of worthy purposes and life's purposes.

Ideally, after birth into this world we should undergo progressive episodes of inner development. Early childhood is the time for getting acquainted with the material realm and learning to adapt. This is the stage during which to be nurtured by parents, and others, and for early education. With puberty and sexual development, we become more conscious of our feelings and instinctual urges and become more interested in the world beyond our former self-centered interests. We perhaps plan for the future, and make decisions which can have a bearing on our lives as adults. As adults, we assume responsibilities, learn to take care of ourselves and our family, and enter into more meaningful social relationships. During late middle years, with family and personal responsibilities settled and with a degree of security assured, we can turn our attention more fully to becoming cultured and in giving back to society some of what society has so generously provided for us. The later years can be used to continue our charitable works as well as to give more personal attention to the completion of our spiritual growth, if this has not already been accomplished. Finally, we should be prepared to depart this world without regret, anticipating continued spiritual awakening and whatever else it may be that our destiny will unfold. This is the ideal progression of human life, but it does not always work out this way.

With alarming frequency human beings experience traumatic mental conflicts and arrested emotional development. I make no sweeping judgments about this; we have only to objectively study the human condition in general to see that this is so. The visible percentage of neurotic and dysfunctional members of society provide evidence to support this observation. And among many who function within the range of what is considered to be normal behavior, I would guess that but a modest percentage are entirely free of mental conflict and emotional confusion. We could blame unsatisfying and even traumatic environmental circumstances which prevailed during the formative years of such persons. We could blame insufficient nurturing, economic hardship, illness, lack of opportunity, parents who did not know how to parent or who did not care to do so, incompetent teachers, lack of suitable role models, the breakup of the domestic environment, alcoholic parents, drug use, and more. Some adults have come through such circumstances, and worse, and are relatively unscarred. Many have been raised in almost ideal circumstances and have made a mess of their lives. Many, also, lead unfulfilled lives because of not having healed the grief, pain, sense of loss, or misunderstandings rooted in childhood years. They have not grown up emotionally, they have not matured sufficiently to function in a healthy-minded way in the adult world.

True, we can be influenced by circumstances. But when we reach the stage in our development where reason and self-determinism can be exercised, when we come to the place where we learn that we can make choices, from that time forward we are responsible for what happens to us: for what we think, how we feel, and how we behave. We can then no longer blame any person or any circumstance of the past for what we inwardly are and what course our life will take.

"Easier said than done," I "hear" someone say, "I've tried to help myself but nothing seems to work." It would be more helpful to say, "It may not be easy but I will educate myself, apply myself, seek out competent help if I need it, and learn to rid my mind of conflicts and discontent. I will become an understanding person and I will experience psychological and spiritual growth until the process of living is easy, natural and spontaneous!" What is needed is the desire, the wanting to wake up, grow up and be able to relate to life as it is.

This means we have to learn to cheerfully, while rising above inner psychological resistance, do the things we have to do to make possible orderly changes and the actualization of our heart's desire. It is only by doing that

On Waking Up

we provide ourselves the opportunity to experience beneficial transformations. How do we want to be? Then, let us be like that. How do we want to think? Let us think like that. How do we want to feel? Let us feel like that. What kind of lifestyle would be most supportive to the attainment of worthy purposes? Let us provide that lifestyle. What do we really want to do with our time and talents in this world? Let us do it.

Most people who are living in a relatively open society are already doing what they want to do. Some of their circumstances and behaviors may seem strange to us, even bizarre, but they have agreed to do the things they are doing. If they did not want to do those things and have those experiences, and if they had the desire to do and experience otherwise, they would make inner adjustments in attitude and consciousness and outer adjustments in relationships and circumstances. They would change their behavior. This is why some teachers of metaphysics say that every person is now perfectly demonstrating in his or her life exactly what his or her mental states are, and what is personally acceptable.

People who are for the most part unconscious, tend to drift with the tides of life, to adapt, to fit in, to cope, to make do, to survive as best they can. People who are a little more awake and in whom subconscious influences are dominant, tend to take a more active interest in life but are subject to making errors in perception and judgment, to fantasy, delusion and escapism. They are often reactive to circumstances, to their own psychological conflicts as well as to outer conditions. People who are more conscious tend to be more self-determined, more reasonable, more goal-oriented, more self-responsible. They may still have some subconscious conflicts and delusions but they tend to be more focused and purposeful. They attempt to be in charge of their lives. People who are more superconscious tend to think in terms of a relationship with God, to naturally be possibility-thinkers, open to inspiration, more generous, healthier, prosperous and functional. They are inclined to feel comfortable living a natural life, are interested in higher philosophical matters and engage in periodic interludes of silence, prayer, meditation, and contemplation. From this stage they can awaken to a sense of cosmic consciousness, an awareness of One Life manifesting as all of Nature and all living things. Such a person may experience occasional or frequent episodes of transcendence and supernatural insight. As a result of superconscious and cosmic conscious awareness, physiological functions are regulated, mental processes are ordered, and relationships and circumstances unfold harmoniously. Grace abounds. Beyond this is God consciousness and full illumination of consciousness.

Physiological development and psychological growth are but the foundations upon which spiritual growth occurs. As spiritual growth progresses, higher (superconscious) influences become increasingly evident at physiological and psychological levels, causing a refinement of the brain, nervous system and body as well as transformations in the mental field. But physical wellness and psychological growth should not be neglected. Our consciousness is processed through mind and body and the more balanced and harmonious are the workings of mind and body, the easier it is for us to express through them.

In referring to gradient levels of awareness I am highlighting the dominant characteristics and influences of each level while being aware of the fact that all levels are somewhat apparent regardless of the dominant characteristics and influences. For instance, a person who is for the most part unaware may have occasions of higher aspiration and intimations of soul awareness. A person who is for the most part influenced by subconscious tendencies may sincerely aspire to be self-responsible and more functional. A person who is reasonably functional and possesses knowledge of how to accomplish purposes may want to outgrow ego-drive and awaken to higher states of consciousness. A person in whom superconscious influences are dominant may still experience episodes of restlessness and inertia. A person with a degree of cosmic consciousness may attempt to confine higher understanding into a traditional religious frame of reference. A person new in God conscious awareness may retain a degree of egocentricity, which will eventually dissolve as complete enlightenment unfolds. Seldom is a person completely stable at any level below the enlightened state. Some "sinners" have saintly qualities and some "saints" may at times doubt their understanding or become painfully aware of inner conditions which need to be confronted and released.

As we progress through the adult stages of our lives, emotional maturity is usually the slowest growth process to be actualized. We may be physically healthy, financially comfortable, reasonably fulfilled in our relationships, educated and cultured, and still be somewhat emotionally immature. We may not yet have come to terms with childhood memories or the hurts and failures experienced since then, or arrived at a satisfying level of understanding of our relationship with God. We may actually choose not to look too closely at the matter of what will become of us when we die to this world. An unexpected illness, financial challenge, a terminated relationship, a forced change in lifestyle, may be devastating to our peace of mind and ruin everything we have worked so diligently to attain.

But even if we live with reasonable dignity, if we die to this world emotionally confused and spiritually unawakened we will not have completed our journey successfully. Therefore, I am advocating *complete* awakening, optimum emotional maturity, and a clear understanding of our relationship with life processes on all levels. *Optimum* here means "most ideal for the accomplishment of our purposes." Complete spiritual awakening will contribute to spontaneous emotional maturity. It is therefore not necessary to solve all psychological problems before committing completely to spiritual growth. Attaining a functional level of emotional maturity will suffice to enable us to aspire to higher states of consciousness and these, in turn, will assist in the integration of the personality and the removal of remaining inner conflicts. We are to help ourselves to be as functional as we can be, while remembering that grace is the saving factor.

Extending Awareness Beyond the Boundaries of Mind and Senses

While it is an obvious convenience in this world to be able to easily express through the mind and senses for the purpose of relating to objective circumstances, it is a considerable inconvenience for one on the awakening path to be restricted to mind and senses. The brain is the physical organ of the non-physical mind. Senses are rooted in the mind and function through the brain and nervous system. Our awareness, however, is not dependent upon mental processes or sensory perceptions for we can be aware without thoughts and mental transformations and without sensory stimulation. During sleep our awareness is unconsciously removed from mental and sensory involvement, and during occasions of transcendent awareness, awareness is consciously removed from mental and sensory involvement. For an aware person the axiom, "I think, therefore I am," is changed to "I am, therefore I am."

During transcendent episodes we become aware of unrestricted and unbounded soul awareness, during which occasions we may experience pure existence without any evidence of modification. We may also experience unrestricted and unbounded soul awareness while being simultaneously aware of the manifest worlds as a play of cosmic forces, as well as many or all subjective realms with their interactions of cosmic forces which underlie physical manifestations. During such occasions one may literally "see all and know all" and later be unable to explain in words what was seen and known. This realization can, at times, be shared with another who is receptive, by a process of direct transmission. This is why some enlightenment traditions recommend that a seeker of knowledge associate with enlightened persons. Inner knowledge as well as states of consciousness can be shared through a process of induction, the transmission of realization from one person to another by nonverbal means.

It is our common experience that we "take on" moods, attitudes, behaviors, and even states of consciousness by association with others. Companionship with people who are more actualized than we are can elevate us to their levels of awareness. If it is not possible to actually enjoy physical association, we can at least "fellowship with the saints" by mentally attuning ourselves with them and to higher states of consciousness. Such attunement will result in constructive changes in attitude, thinking, emotional states, and behavior.

To occasionally visit religious shrines, places of higher learning and cultural centers can be soul elevating. To occasionally enjoy the company of spiritually dedicated friends can be helpful. To arrange our personal environment so that it is supportive, is certainly helpful. In my office where I write and work, I have photographs of saints and of people whose lives are an inspiration to me. Whatever we can do to ensure that our minds are nourished with quality influences, is helpful.

Because of our mental conditionings and our habitual ways of viewing our world, we are usually limited in what we can see and comprehend. A person functioning at a strongly conditioned level of awareness may not be able to imagine how it would be to be able to see from a higher level, or to imagine the possibility of being able to function without limitations. A person who is more aware and somewhat soul actualized may wonder why others prefer their lives of obvious limitation and sometimes misery. A sick person may not be able to imagine being well. A poor person may not be able to imagine being affluent. A lonely person may not be able to imagine having a loving relationship. A traditionally minded religious person may not be able to imagine the existence of a benevolent Power which nourishes the universe. Except when grace intervenes, or the accumulated psychic forces we have set into motion because of past efforts result in occasions of breakthrough, our psychological and spiritual growth is usually slow. We may aspire to only modest improvement: small improvement in health, a margin of improvement in understanding, a little more emotional maturity, perhaps a glimmer of insight—not too much, but enough to make life better than it presently is.

We may, because of a desire to improve our lifestyle, somewhat modify our behavior. We may lose weight, add an exercise routine to our daily regimen, be more attentive to the selection of food we eat, make a little better use of our time and resources, make an effort to improve our understanding, make an appointment with a psychotherapist, attend self-help seminars and even explore the possibilities of meditation and spiritual growth. Any of these procedures, and others which may be useful can be helpful, but our long-term purposeful involvement is the deciding factor. Why do we do these things? Is it so we can be like other people we know who are doing these things? Or is it because we sincerely want to unfold our inner potential and experience all we can be? Any inner vision of possibilities which we attempt to actualize is useful. Best of all, is an inner vision of all things possible because this will ensure that we do not settle for partial growth and marginal improvement. The ideal is to experience all we can be, within the framework of present limitations. Then, go beyond limitations.

A woman once wrote to inform me that she was "now enlightened after having attended a ten-hour growth seminar" and that her spiritual journey was concluded. I have met many people who professed to "being saved" whose behavior and circumstances did not reflect their claimed condition, and others who now "know the truth" because of having completed a few months of metaphysical studies during which they learned to use their mental abilities to "be in control of their destiny." I also know some who are self-righteously complacent because they "have a guru who is enlightened," and do little or nothing

Extending Awareness

to contribute to their own continued psychological and spiritual growth.

Even when we become accomplished in the use of mental principles of causation (which we should), inner wisdom dictates that we should also be open to further expansion of consciousness so that we unfold the capacity to experience the transition from law to grace, from forever needing to cause effects to learning to allow them to unfold spontaneously. We then experience that while we still do our part in creative endeavors, we are led from within to make right choices: to act when necessary and to rest when necessary, to exercise will (gentle, focused intention) when necessary and to "let go and let God" when necessary. Learning to function from this higher level of consciousness is as different from the level of using the mechanics of mental causation as that level differs from the level of personal physical effort.

At the level of physical effort only, we may think in terms of, "It's me and the world and I have to do everything myself." At the level of proficiency in the use of laws of mental causation we may think, "I am the master of my fate." At the level from which grace is spontaneously operational we know, "I am a bubble of consciousness in the Ocean of life and everything happens according to Its will." At the physical level we may think of death of the body as the end of us, or perhaps a transition to realms about which we have no clear understanding. At the metaphysical level, we may think of death of the physical body as a departure from this world and entry into higher levels of awareness and continued expression. At the level of real knowledge we understand that we may continue on to subtle realms to further our spiritual unfoldment or we may experience transcendence when ego-sense is dissolved.

Occasional experiences of extended awareness may result in our being able to know things intuitively, without sensory support. We may do this frequently without paying too much attention to the process. We may know who is calling when the telephone rings. We may know that a letter or parcel is on the way to us. We may have a knack for being at the right place at the most opportune time, easily find parking places, or find items we desire to purchase at the first store we go to. We may be able to know solutions to problems. Our reading comprehension may be excellent and effortless. We may have occasions of precognition, of knowing ahead of time what is to happen on the personal scene or elsewhere in the world. We may have telepathic and precogitive dreams. We may be able to think of a person and know their thoughts and circumstances.

Some people have inner faculties so well developed that they can do these things, and more, at will. They may be able to see with inner vision events occurring at locations remote from them. They may be able to see into someone else's mind or body and diagnose underlying conditions which are supporting outer symptoms of disease and psychological unrest. Some can comprehend the subjective levels of Nature and discern inner workings of the universe. Some can see into the heart of Reality and know the source of manifest life.

Experimentation with these abilities for the purpose of expanding awareness and improving function, can be helpful. Over-fascination with them and becoming preoccupied to the extent that spiritual growth is neglected, can be detrimental. Occasional episodes of extrasensory perception can be useful because they may prove to us that we are indeed more than mind or body. We may then be inspired to explore the possibilities of acquiring higher knowledge leading to soul actualization. Many people who have witnessed (or experienced) spontaneous healing, dramatic changes in circumstances for the better, and even instances of the materialization of physical objects by an exercise of focused intention, have had their lives immediately changed for the better as a result. They have seen with their own eyes that the physical universe is not solid and unyielding at all, but is fluid and subject to transformation when inner causes are adjusted.

Miracles are in the Eye of the Beholder

Many of the circumstances we take for granted in our everyday experience might be considered miraculous to a person who has had no prior awareness of them. Some of our ancestors trekked for months across the western plains of America to reach their destinations. We now journey from New York City to Los Angeles in five hours flying time. Radio and television brings us news of events as they occur from any part of the world. Medical advances have eliminated many diseases. Explorations into spirit-mind-body relationships are in progress and we are "discovering" that spiritual awareness is superior to mental and physical processes when right understanding and intention are present. We know that possibility-thinking and controlled imagination can determine physical outcomes. We know that spiritual growth can be accelerated. We know that human physiology can be altered, the brain and nervous system refined so that consciousness can more easily be processed, and that our common relationships with the world are dependent upon how we view it and ourselves. These are not really miracles, they are expressions of the utilization of available inner resources in harmony with natural laws of causation.

In our sleeping dreams we can fly through the air without mechanical means, communicate with friends in this world and others, manipulate the elements, and even experience expanded states of awareness—no longer constrained by limitations usually associated with sensory relationships. We can also do many of these things in the waking state, when we know we can. All of our limitations are caused by restricted states of consciousness and our lack of knowledge of how to implement useful changes. When we awaken spiritually our soul abilities also unfold, allowing us freedom to express as we are meant to express. When inner restricting conditions are eliminated, outer circumstances improve.

What is your vision of possibilities? How far can you see with your mind's eye, with inner vision? How high can you soar? What do you anticipate for yourself a week from now, a year from now, or as far as you can presently see? Yours for the imagining, the believing, accepting and actualizing are the gifts of all things possible.

TWO

Living in God

God has given man the eye of investigation by which he may see and recognize truth. He has endowed man with ears that he may hear the message of reality, and conferred upon him the gift of reason by which he may discover things for himself. Man is not intended to see through the eyes of another, hear through another's ears nor comprehend with another's brain. Each human creature has individual endowment, power and responsibility in the creative plan of God.
ABDUL BAHA (1844-1921)
The Mysterious Forces of Civilization

From all which I conclude, there is a Mind which affects me every moment with all the sensible impressions I perceive. And, from the variety, order, and manner of these, I conclude the Author of them to be wise, powerful, and good beyond comprehension. Mark it well; I do not say, I see things by perceiving that which represents them in the intelligible Substance of God. This I do not understand: but I say, the things by me perceived are known by the understanding, and produced by the will of an infinite Spirit.
GEORGE BERKELEY (1685-1753)
Three Dialogues

Let us not content ourselves with loving God for the mere sensible favors, however elevated, which He has done or may do us. Such favors, though never so great, cannot bring us so near to Him as faith does in one simple act.
BROTHER LAWRENCE (1605-1691)
The Practice of the Presence of God

When I asked people to share with me their understanding and feelings about God*, their responses were revealing. Many affirmed their personal understanding of God and their conviction of having a good relationship with God. Some admitted that their awareness of God "comes and goes" and a few said they sometimes neglect thinking about God until they have a problem. Several said, "My ego often gets in the way, but I'm working on this." Some other comments were:

"I was raised in a Christian fundamentalist environment and I have difficulty thinking of God as being a loving God."

"Is God personal or impersonal? If personal, how really personal and caring? If impersonal, why do I still feel like praying to God?"

"My concept of God is elusive: sometimes almost clear and sometimes not clear at all."

"If God is the original expansion from the field of pure consciousness, is God a 'big soul' and am I a 'little soul?' "

"I am afraid of God because of what God allows in the world. In fact, when I think about it I am filled with cold dread."

"I think all this talk about God is nonsense."

"If God is all, and I am part of God, why am I not God?"

"How can I know the difference between God's will and my will? And what is God's will for us?"

* See the Introduction

"For the moment, at least, I have turned from God because my mother's prayers weren't answered."

"My feelings about God change. How can I reconcile my occasional insights about God as an omnipresent being, versus my need for God as a loving father?"

"I find it hard to believe in God when I am depressed or discouraged."

"I blame my childhood exposure to incorrect teachings about God for my present confusion and unrest."

I think almost all of us can relate to these comments. We share the same conditions, feelings and aspirations. We share the same challenges and growth episodes. So let us, together, explore this matter of God and our relationship to God and see if our understanding can be improved and our spiritual growth quickened.

The One Relationship that Makes All Others Worthwhile

Every illumined spiritual teacher has said it—and in our heart (our being) we know it's true—that it is possible to experience a conscious relationship with God and that we must do it if we are to be fulfilled. But how do we do this? What can we do to help ourselves know God and live in a knowing relationship with God? Can we all really do it? Are some more fortunate than others because they seem to do this so easily? And how can we reconcile the assertion that "God is good" when confronted at every turn by personal challenge and outer evidence of imperfect conditions on the world scene? Is our religious impulse merely a neurotic inclination to deny our immortality? Do we yearn for a vague, somewhat satisfying relationship with a cosmic father or mother figure because we are really emotionally immature and in need of parental reassurance—for someone to take care of us because we

The One Worthwhile Relationship

feel so alone and incapable of caring for ourselves? Are we seeking a hoped-for relationship with God because our human relationships are so barren or because our present relationship with the world is so incomplete? And why is it, that even when we are sincere in our yearning to know God, we seem to make so little progress in experiencing the fulfillment of our heart's desire?

If we are healthy-minded, we want more than a mild degree of assurance that God is real and occasional indications that divine intervention can occur. What we really want is an eminent God—a conspicuous, prominent, projecting, protruding (into our personal space and time), expressing God. We want a now-manifestation of God in our lives as fact. And how would such a relationship with God be for us? It would mean that we would experience life as natural, joyous and spontaneous. That we would be healthy, happy, knowledgeable, emotionally mature, on friendly terms with everyone and everything, successful in our worthy ventures, selfless, ever about God's will, easily having at our disposal whatever was needed to satisfy our needs and to accomplish our purposes and be in the flow of grace. It would mean that we would be completely spiritually awake.

Well, God *is* eminent and all of these evidential expressions of God here-and-now are ours for learning how to be open to them. (Ask yourself, "If someone with the ability to do so, offered me complete understanding of God and all of the results of that understanding, would I say 'yes' to the invitation?") What is obviously needed, if God-knowledge and God-relationship is not presently being experienced, is for us to learn what God really is and how to open ourselves to accept what is presently available.

The hard truth is that even if we assert that we are open and accepting and results are not apparent, we obviously are not yet capable of acknowledging (seeing) and actualizing (experiencing in fact) what is now being demonstrated by others who are truly open and accepting. We may need to learn how to live more in harmony with natural and metaphysical laws. We may need to rid ourselves of confusion and conflict. We may need to be willing to dissolve the boundaries of ego consciousness. We may need to release restricting attitudes and beliefs. We may need to stop feeling unworthy and get out of personality and into soul awareness. We may need to release attachments to things and circumstances and be courageous and adventuresome enough to allow consciousness to expand. We may need to rid ourselves of the habit of procrastination and do something positive and constructive for ourselves. We may need to start living as consciously and competently as we can, in order to learn by doing and prepare ourselves for further growth.

The one relationship that makes all others worthwhile is our relationship with God. With it, all other relationships are enriched. Without it, all other relationships will not satisfy because they, of themselves, cannot. All relationships except soul to God relationships are effects of inner causes and are, therefore, constantly undergoing transformations and changes. Being effects, they can provide temporary support but they cannot be relied upon to forever persist. But *that* which makes possible all outer circumstances, persists, and makes possible continuing unfoldments of circumstances. This is why it is taught that we should turn to the giver of gifts, the source of all manifestation, if we would know changeless inner peace and complete soul fulfillment. Grasping at relationships and forever striving to achieve goals to provide meaning to life is the outer way, the way of certain frustration, because that outer relationship or circumstance upon which we become dependent is illusory.

With even partial knowledge of God, and partial awareness of God *as* the fabric of the world, we can learn to live from a conscious realization of being-now and having-now instead of thinking in terms of becoming or acquiring. *What we are, as being, is as real and permanent as God is real and permanent. What we have, in consciousness, can manifest outwardly as increased understanding and as appropriate circumstances supportive of our high purposes.* This is the esoteric meaning of the New Testament scripture verse (*The Gospel According to Saint Luke* 19:26): "...to every one who has, shall be given; and from him that has not, even that which he has (outwardly) shall be taken away from him." That which we experience in consciousness increases in expression; but incomplete or imperfect realization of having, tends to result in a diminishing of obvious indications. This is why it is essential, when we desire a relationship with God, for us to feel right about it and to be able to fully accept it. And when we desire physical health, mental proficiency, psychological wellness, supportive relationships, success in ventures—anything worthy of us—that we be established in the consciousness, the soul conviction, of already having it.

Our lives are different when we live from higher understanding. "Not at all similar are the race of the immortal gods and the race of men who walk upon the earth," wrote Homer*. In some cultures those who have outgrown conditioned states of consciousness are referred to as gods and goddesses, souls who have awakened from the "dream of mortality" and its complexities. A spiritually awake person views the world more clearly and experiences life accordingly, though the difference may not always be obvious to others who do not share his perceptions. The pain and confusion that was present before spiritual awakening fades away. Even memories of a perhaps burdensome journey to discovery may dissolve without a trace.

The Primary Importance of Complete Spiritual Education for Every Person

The almost total neglect of the average person's spiritual education is appalling and reflects not only widespread ignorance, but a pervasive lack of interest in

---

* *The Iliad*, circa 700 B.C., Greece.

matters other than those which serve immediate personal concerns. While the religious impulse is innate to us, rationality in exploring higher and ultimate possibilities is often transparently absent. The tendency then, of many, is to settle for a comfortable understanding of life processes, one sufficient to provide only a degree of emotional satisfaction.

Spiritual education should begin with an examination of first causes, of the nature of consciousness and how, from it, the objective realms unfold. Once it is understood that we are spiritual beings, able to cooperate with natural, universal forces which govern all life processes, we are then in a position to live as we are intended to live. We will know our origins, our true nature as spiritual beings, our relationship with God and Nature and what future possibilities await us in this and other realms. Without this understanding, we are inclined to believe ourselves to be physical beings confined to a few decades of uncertain circumstances.

It would be well for children to be accurately informed about the facts of life during their early years. Most children have no difficulty in accepting (and to a considerable degree, understanding) how the universe works when they are informed in a straightforward manner. Adults often have difficulty in becoming spiritually educated because of ego-resistance, difficulties in relating newly presented valid information to already formed attitudes and opinions, and because they fear change. Many adults are already "so skillful in their ignorance" that their rationality is bounded (their ability to exercise intelligence is restricted). Only intelligent, moral and well qualified persons should teach children to ensure that adult prejudices and errors in judgment are not communicated.

Our conditioned social behaviors and habits, along with varying degrees of intellectual incapacity or laziness, are often the major reasons for our inability to learn easily and to experience psychological and spiritual growth.

How Can We Know What is True?

We know the truth about anything when we have accurate information about it. A truth seeker is a person who is committed to understanding. When we really understand the reality of God and our relationship with God, our knowledge and experience are expressed in our lives. This is how we can know if we are "of the truth," our lives bear witness to our understanding.

Can anyone who is reasonably intelligent understand the nature of God and have a relationship with God? Of course. Even if profound intelligence is lacking, so long as there is a desire to experience a relationship with God, it can be experienced. The reason for this is that we are spiritual beings, already grounded in God, so the relationship already exists. What is needed is for us to consciously know this.

The recommended approach to higher knowledge is for one to live as harmoniously as possible with the laws of Nature; that is, do all that is possible to be a good, moral human being. Along with doing this, cultivate devotion and desire to know God. Devotion diminishes egoism, attunes the soul to divine qualities, awakens spiritual forces, purifies the intellect and awakens intuition. Sincere desire helps in focusing our inner capacities, provides motivation for disciplined behavior and attracts to us that which is desired. There must also be a willingness to learn—and to allow convictions, attitudes and behaviors to change in the light of new discovery and as a result of inner transformation which is certain to occur.

Take on faith what knowledgeable people assert to be true, then test your understanding in the classroom of daily application and experience. It is well to be a student of a master, but the ideal is to become like the master.

When spiritual consciousness is present, ability to

comprehend spiritual matters is natural. When we are mentally healthy, life is enjoyable and neurosis is absent. When wellness-consciousness is present, we are physically well. When we are emotionally mature, we are self-responsible. When we acknowledge our own innate goodness and the innate goodness of others, supportive relationships are established and maintained. When we are on harmonious terms with the universe, we prosper in all ways and the universe supports us. When we are on purpose in life, life has meaning. These signs are evidence of actualizing the truth of what we know.

God, the World and Us

The word *God* has Sanskrit language origins and comes to us through Germanic and Old English languages. An ancestor word *hu* is found in the *Rig Veda* (presently the oldest known religious scripture) and refers to "the one who is invoked," or whose influence is invited into human affairs. But just *what* or, *who*, is God? According to seers who claim to know, God is the first expansion or outward manifestation from a field of pure consciousness. This field of pure consciousness is that from which God unfolds and from God, everything else comes into expression by a process of self-referral; since consciousness is exclusive (there being nothing but it in existence) it can only relate to itself. This is why (when we learn to speak the "language") we say the universe and everything manifesting in it, is consciousness manifesting-as.

The varied expressions of consciousness this side of the Godhead are but categories of manifestation, not created manifestations separate from the Godhead. The Godhead is also referred to as the Oversoul. When considered to be influential to universal (and personal) processes, the Godhead is often referred to as the Lord or ruler. Within the Godhead are three influential aspects, the results of

God, the World and Us

polarity, which further express through the universe. These are referred to as the attributes of luminosity (pure essence), movement (which makes possible happenings) and inertia (which makes possible objective manifestation). When these three attributes are in a condition of equilibrium God exists but the universe does not. When they stir, a vibrational creative force (Om, Aum, the Word) flows into expression and begins the process of universal manifestation. Since the creative force is inseparable from God, and the universe is inseparable from the creative force, we say that God, the creative force and the field of Nature, are one.

For convenience, the Godhead is referred to as male and the creative force and its manifestations as female. So some people refer to God, as Father, and to God-as-Nature, as Mother.

From the field of God, then, the universe emerges as a creative force, aspects of the creative force described as not-quite-matter, subatomic particles, atoms, molecules and the full range of manifestations of consciousness-as-matter we behold about us.

Supreme consciousness always knows itself. The process of knowing the objective side of self-manifestation resulted in the expression of a cosmic or universal mind. So there is the knower, the process of knowing, and the known, all contained within the field of God.

Souls are units of consciousness, as God is, but these specialized souls are not the Oversoul. We came from the source, through the field of God, but are here to participate with God, not to replace God. We can become God-like, we can merge in God and we can transcend the attributes of God to experience pure or absolute being. While in relative awareness we do well to remember our relationship with God and what our role is in relationship with God. We are here to cooperate with God's will, the process of evolution, until it is our destiny to merge in God and experience transcendence. Not only can we do this, sooner or later we will learn to do it. We may, in our self-centered moments, wish it were otherwise, but it isn't. That's how the cosmic game-plan is set up.

Just as there is a cosmic mind, so there are individualized minds, which are formed of cosmic mind-stuff. These are our minds: yours, mine, and every other person's (and creature's). Our identification with the mind results in ego-sense, which has been called the major error of the intellect. Assuming ourselves to be independent units of awareness we then tend to become attached to externals: to mental processes and if embodied, to the nervous system, sense urges, and the objects of the senses. Often so strong is this identification that we falsely assume ourselves to be mortal creatures subject to birth, causation and death. This is the delusion from which we have to awaken.

Delusion suppresses intuition and clouds the intellect, making it difficult for us to be rational and to determine the truth about ourselves and our world. Delusion gives rise to errors in perception and errors in judgment, resulting in an illusory view of the world. The world is not an illusion because it is a manifestation of cosmic forces, but our misperception of it forms the basis of our illusions. Spiritual awakening results in purification of the intellect, which makes accurate determination possible and the unveiling of intuition which enables us to perceive directly, without reliance upon the senses.

Inefficient use of intellect and the consequent errors in judgment, along with unregulated sense urges, create conflicts in the mental field and cause emotional unrest. Thus confusion and blind involvement with life processes follow. Without the exercise of intelligence, without sensory impulses being regulated, one tends to experience increasing difficulties and an accumulation of memories, traumas, desires, and mental and emotional conflicts. This results in a conditioned-condition in which one lives for the most part unconsciously. This condition is considered quite normal for human beings. Don't take my word for it, just go out and look around.

Why did God create the world? Simple-minded philosophers sometimes say that "God was lonely and created the world to keep himself company." I've actually heard people say that! The plain truth is, when the three attributes within the Godhead are unbalanced, the creation process begins. After a duration of trillions of solar years, a duration of non-manifestation occurs. Manifestation and non-manifestation are referred to as the outbreathing and inbreathing of God*.

How to Walk and Talk with God

When we think about God, pray to God or otherwise attempt to experience a relationship with God, regardless of the thoughts or words we use or the reasonable approach we make, our soul aspiration is the deciding factor. Surrendered aspiration awakens soul capacities and attracts divine influences into our mind and consciousness.

A problem many traditionally religious people have is that of removing their awareness from distracting memories which are the result of prior conditioning and the acquisition of misinformation. They may, for instance, still be thinking of God as a cosmic person who keeps a record of their every thought and action and who rewards or punishes accordingly. They may still be thinking of God as a judgmental, even wrathful being. They may feel that they have to believe in a prescribed creed or that they must, if they are to be worthy of God's grace, profess their faith in one or more of God's representatives or special manifestations. That such assumptions are erroneous has not prevented their being taught and believed for multiplied thousands of years.

If we feel God to be a cosmic parent, we may behave in childish ways, hoping to please him or attempting to avoid his observation because of our feelings of guilt and unwor-

---

* For a more extensive commentary on the categories of cosmic manifestation see the author's book *Life Surrendered in God*. CSA Press, Lakemont, Georgia.

thiness. We may even be afraid of God. If our prayers are not answered in the way we would like for them to be, we may feel that God does not love us. If we have been conditioned to believe that God can only be approached through a specific traditional religious system, we may remain narrow-minded, even self-righteous, oblivious of the fact that many sincere devotees have experienced a relationship with God without any formal sectarian affiliation.

We can never "find God" in a contrived belief system. A Christian, Hindu, Buddhist, Jew, Moslem, or anyone who has chosen to accept a spiritual growth path within the framework of any traditional religious discipline, may experience spiritual growth and eventual God-realization as a result of self-discipline aided by the support of a community of believers—but higher stages of growth will result in the transcendence of non-useful beliefs and practices. A spiritually evolved person may certainly choose to remain identified with a traditional religious system of philosophical study and practice, because of the support that it provides and to ensure its continued availability to others who might benefit by association.

The Latin root from which the word *religion* comes means "to bind." Like the Sanskrit word *yoga* (of which one meaning is "to yoke" or "to bring together"), religion is for the purpose of restoring one's attention to changeless Reality. It is not for the purpose of restricting personal growth, it is for the purpose of helping us become all we can be—to experience all things possible. All meaningful religious (or yogic) discipline and practice is for the purpose of liberating soul consciousness.

Christ (Greek *christos*, "anointed," translation of the Hebrew word for "messiah") consciousness is the aspect of God consciousness eminent in creation, in the field of Nature. For an informed Christian, "to be in Christ" is to be identified with this aspect of God. "To be in Christ" is to be other than a conditioned personality. Various names have been given to this aspect of consciousness, which is just as impersonal, yet personal to one who experiences it, as God is both impersonal yet personal.

So long as we understand that our concept (and experience) of God serves our spiritual growth, we need have no conflicts about considering ourselves in a personal relationship with God. (Problems can arise, however, if we unwisely attempt to convert others to our point of view.) If our approach to God is predominately devotional we will usually feel more comfortable in relating to God in a personal way. We can be devoted to the impersonal, formless Reality but this may require more understanding and faith than the average spiritual novice has in the early stages of his study and practice. It is the testimony of many people, of different times and cultures, that "a caring presence" is able to manifest itself and that it often intervenes and directs the course of human affairs. Contemplatives whose avowed purpose was to know the changeless Reality beyond name and form have confessed to experiencing, on the inward journey, communication with benevolent presences and, finally, an awareness of a Being of light in whom they felt themselves dissolving. (Some seers say that even this relationship will eventually be surpassed.)

Is it possible to walk and talk with God? Yes, it is possible. It is possible to live our lives in an awareness of God's reality and to relate to it. This is done by acknowledging the presence even before it is actually experienced, by surrendering to behaviors which are appropriate to such a relationship and by being quietly alert to indications that the relationship is developing. No matter what you are doing, no matter how conditions in your life presently are, know that behind the screen of your mind and behind the appearances of the world around you, there is that which exists without which nothing could exist. Know that behind your thoughts and moods, at the level of being, your nature is pure existence, the pure existence aspect of Reality supports you and its varying expressive aspects nourish and guide you. It may occur slowly, or it may occur suddenly, but eventually you will vividly experience a relationship with something bigger than you, wiser than you are. The fruits of your relationship with God will be soul peace, blessed assurance, a heightened moral sense, a sense of purpose and direction in life, and psychological and spiritual growth. If these signs do not follow, your presumption of such a conscious relationship is illusory. Or it may be that a degree of God-awareness is present but has not yet become sufficiently operational to result in inner transformation.

While illusions are not always easily dispelled, it is well for us to be as clear-minded as possible and avoid excursions into fantasy. A reoccurring phenomenon among certain groups in society is that of curious involvement with procedures presumed to enable one to communicate with spiritually advanced beings from other realms. It is, of course, possible to have telepathic communication with other people in this and, other, spheres and to enjoy a spiritual rapport unsupported by the senses often referred to as having "fellowship with the saints." But what I here refer to is a practice which used to be widely known as spiritualism or mediumship, and surfaced during the decade of the nineteen-eighties as "channeling." Emotionally immature, spiritually unawakened people will often grasp at practices that remotely seem to provide quick access to higher understanding and immediate personal improvement. They are then easily mislead and sink into further episodes of self-delusion. Every enlightened person I know counsels against the practice of mediumship in every form. Illumined souls simply do not speak (or write) through human beings who are otherwise unexceptional in their understanding or behavior.

"There where the creature ends, God begins to be. God does not ask anything of you other than you go out of yourself according to your mode as a creature and that you let God be God in you," wrote Meister Eckhart almost 700 years ago. The "creature" is the human condition which is to be transcended if we are to actually consciously experience a relationship with God. A devotional hymn loved by many Christians has the words: "And He walks with me and He talks with me, and He tells me I am His own, and the joy we share as we tarry there, none other has ever known." It is a common feeling, of persons who experience an awareness of the presence of God, that it is special and even unlike anything anyone else has ever experienced. It is somewhat like being in love; we may acknowledge that other people have known love, but our love experience must surely be unique. Devotees who claim an intimate relationship with God testify to its sweetness and satisfying permanency.

It is my experience that Meister Eckhart was correct when he wrote about the going out of ourselves (out of the conditioned state) as being necessary if the reality of God is to be apprehended. Even the intellect must be transcended because subtle and fine matters are only accessible by intuition. One need not be intellectually developed in order to experience a relationship with God, although intellect has value in enabling us to better understand this-world relationships and processes. The intellect can even enable us to understand, to a considerable degree, the subjective side of life. But the intellectual faculty, being of the mind, cannot reveal to us what is beyond it.

A seeming-distance between us and God is due to our own inability to be aware of what is true about God, ourselves and the world. It is one thing to intellectually accept that God is the only Being, Life, Power and Substance; it is another to train ourselves to feel, see and know this. Often our sense of being apart from God is due to faulty thinking—we may continue to think of God as being beyond us, beyond the field of Nature, somehow present but elusive.

What is unfolding on the world scene (and in our daily relationships and circumstances) is due to the ceaseless movements of cosmic forces which have their origins in the Godhead. Wherever there is discord, there is evidence of evolutionary change and a need on our part to adjust our attitude—and our behavior if discord is affecting us in some way. The metaphysical view of life is that everything is occurring in the field of cosmic mind. Just as our day-to-day and moment-to-moment perceptions and experiences exist in the realm of imagination, so the universe is an imaginal phenomenon; it is taking place in cosmic mind.

By *imagination* I do not mean that circumstances are unreal, only that they are illusory and effects of underlying causes. Because we are not always conscious of our deeper drives, our desires and inclinations, and because we do not always remember the thoughts and attitudes (and perhaps, behaviors) which are resulting in the present manifesting circumstances, we may feel that we are almost always the effect of causes external to ourselves. Sometimes we are, because we share the human condition with the rest of the world population and we can also be influenced by forces operating in collective consciousness. With practice, we can learn to make inner adjustments in states of consciousness, mental attitude, conviction and will, and introduce desired changes into our lives and into planetary consciousness.

Social conditions, for instance, reflect the states of consciousness—which determine mental states and behavior—of individuals as well as local, national and global populations. Beneficial changes introduced by one person can influence the circumstances of everyone else. This is why individual spiritual growth is so important. Our light, lights the world to the degree that we are conscious. But world conditions are not entirely dependent upon the states of consciousness and mental states of human beings—there is an evolutionary force presently influential which is contributing to rapid changes and the collective spiritual growth of humanity. This is not to say that we are on the verge of an era of universal enlightenment, for we are not, but we are in the dawning of that era.

To walk and talk with God, cultivate self-confidence: soul-confidence. If we can believe the varied reports which frequently appear in the secular press (and we probably can, because we know of similar circumstances among our own circle of acquaintances) many people in today's society are insecure, fearful, inept, confused, lonely, and frustrated. Even among those who attempt to improve their condition, efforts are frequently superficial. Many are struggling, often sincerely and sometimes not so sincerely, to "be somebody" or to "amount to something." They want to have a feeling of self-worth, or perhaps a feeling of being loved. Many want to be happy but their psychological conflicts weigh them down and dominate their thoughts and behavior so that they "get in their own way" by sabotaging their otherwise constructive efforts. Many need to learn how to be prosperous but they are afraid of success. Many are sick and are not able to help themselves to wellness because they are confused, ill-informed, or because of a not-so-unconscious desire to withdraw from the world scene because they find it so challenging, so unfulfilling.

And in the arena of spiritual questing, many carry their emotional problems with them and attempt to improve their human condition by a study of metaphysics or by engaging in random, or more intense, routines and practices. The following exchange was observed at a gathering of spiritual aspirants when two persons met after a long separation. The first person said, "Why, you haven't changed in all the years we've been apart!" The other said, "I know. I'm just as crazy as I ever was!"

With self-confidence there will be self-acceptance. Speak the following words aloud, with feeling and conviction:

> I accept myself as a specialized expression of God's consciousness. Because I am a specialized expression of God's consciousness, all of the qualities and capacities of God are within me. I am self-confident, resolved to unfold my innate capacities, and willing to live with purpose from this moment forward.

[Did you actually speak those world aloud? Not once, but several times? If you didn't, before reading any further, return to the affirmation and do it right.]

Now, with self-confidence, proceed. In confidence and faith, do all of the things you know you ought to do and renounce all *thoughts, feelings, actions* and *relationships* which are in no way useful to your higher purposes.

Think of God all of the time. Meditate daily and commune in the spirit. Feed your mind with constructive ideas by reading basic and authoritative spiritual literature. Regulate your thoughts and interior conversations. Be inwardly soul-content and in this way harmonize your emotional life. Perform intentional, result-producing actions. Do your part to nourish relationships by being appropriate and refuse to maintain relationships which are destructive. Either do your part to heal the relationship or remove yourself from it, with love and good will. If you are "hanging around" with people who are not on a constructive course in life, you will almost certainly be negatively influenced. Especially for a novice on the spiritual path, association is often stronger than will power. We may have good intentions, but if we choose to associate with people who are content to remain in conditioned states of consciousness we can easily become like them—or find ourselves "playing their psychological games" in order to maintain a dependent relationship. To do this, is a mistake.

Walk with God by acknowledging that God's life is your life, that God is the life of everyone and every creature and that God is right where you are as the substance of the world and the nourishing energies coursing through it. Talk with God by keeping your mind free of mental static and by being open to insight and guidance. As you become increasingly cosmic conscious, your awareness will expand in the direction of omnipresence. This is how to walk and talk with God. Notice, as time passes, how you are guided to do the right things and to make right choices. Notice how opportunities are presented to you. Notice how problems are solved more easily. Notice how easily you overcome challenges. Notice your increasing inner calm and peace of mind. Notice how loving and patient you are. Notice now miracles small and large (they are the same to God) happen in your life.

You can relate to God however God is real to you. If you feel God to be a Cosmic Reality, then be open to God in that aspect. If you feel God to be a caring Being, then be open to God accordingly. If you are not clear in your mind about what God is, or do not have a soul-sense about God, feel that you are walking and talking with God anyway and your understanding of God will improve.

What is definitely not useful is to deny the existence of God. Similarly not useful is to "believe in" God but to continue to feel unworthy or incapable of communing with God.

If it were announced in your community that God was going to manifest a body and be available at a public meeting, would you not immediately make plans to be there? Or would you miss out on your chance to meet God because of a conflict of engagements? Well, you can meet God more obviously every day, when you meditate.

After you pray and meditate, let your inner calm and awareness of God carry over into your active hours. Don't just pray and run away. Let your inner awareness be integrated into your life so that psychological growth occurs along with spiritual growth. This is important, because often we can inwardly "feel spiritual" but not express much in the way of useful psychological change or useful improvements in circumstances.

Psychological unrest, illness, difficulties of various kinds, are not due to God's disinterest in us: and certainly God does not test us when such circumstances prevail.

I knew a person, years ago, who was considered by many to be a saint (and she did have "saintly" qualities), who also experienced physical distress and pain because of persistent arthritis. Some said her condition was "God's test" to see if her love for God would endure—which, of course, is nonsense. The simple fact was that no one in her life knew how to cure the disease. Had she known how to use natural means and make inner psychological adjustments, along with improved spiritual understanding, she could have been healed. The matter of which the body is formed is subject to higher influences because innate intelligence governs fine forces which determine matter's expression. Some said her condition was karmic. Well, every condition is karmic—every condition has a corresponding cause—but causes can be changed to result in predictable changes in outer effects. (Those who said her condition was karmic were hinting that its cause was related to a prior incarnation.)

Perhaps you have heard someone say,"I feel God's presence, I walk and talk with God, and I am a good person. But I still don't get the things I want." The metaphysical truth is that we always get the things (the circumstances) we consciously or *unconsciously* attract to ourselves. Sometimes what we humanly want is not what providence has in store for us. We may then be outwardly successful but inwardly unfulfilled. Or we may do our best to chart our course in life, only to discover that life has other plans which, when they unfold, are always better than we could have contrived.

Saint John of the Cross (1542-1591) wrote: "The soul lives by that which it loves rather than in the body it animates. For it has not life in the body, but rather gives it to the body and lives in that which it loves." We are like this when we are fully conscious—we, as souls, enliven our bodies but we live in God, our first love.

But, What About the Evil in the World?

An often asked question is, "If God is good, if God is love, why does God allow evil in the world?"

A dictionary reference provides the following information: *Evil* is that which is in violation of or is inconsistent with moral law; harmful, injurious, characterized or accompanied by misfortune or suffering; that which interferes with what is good.

A few people have told me, "I don't believe in God because if God existed, there would be no evil in the world. There would be no suffering, no death, no wars, no crime, no ignorance." Those statements reveal ignorance of the operations of the universe, but it is excusable ignorance. On the other hand, there are many people, past and present, who were once upset by the fact of pain and misfortune so obviously experienced by large numbers of human beings (and creatures), and they did something about it. They searched and studied and meditated, until they were so sufficiently possessed of understanding about the processes of life that their ignorance was replaced by wisdom.

Here is what they discovered. The universe is the result of interactions of cosmic forces. A compelling, transforming and purposeful force is inexorably moving to order the universe and to awaken souls. A force necessary for the outward manifestation of material realms, influences what it relates to with its inertia. In religious literature these forces are symbolically referred to as the forces of light and of darkness. Science understands them to be necessary if the universe is to be manifested and expressive. However, when we do not understand cosmic processes and, instead, ask simplistic questions about good and evil from our limited perspective, we tend to reduce the question to "Why does God allow things to be as they are?" Since the universe is a drama of cosmic forces occurring in the field of cosmic mind, everything is occurring within God's consciousness. So a more focused question—instead of "Why does God allow it"—might be, "What is happening, and why?"

At a less than cosmic level of understanding we are naturally sometimes troubled by what we experience and what we see happening in the world. We don't like war. We don't like poverty. We don't like to see people going hungry. We don't like crime. We don't like the fact that people get sick and die. We don't like a lot of things. And we shouldn't like them. But there is something we can do to remove ourselves from these processes and perhaps show others how to be removed from them. It has to do with understanding, spiritual growth and behavior. These are not always as easy to facilitate as it is to complain about why God allows misfortune.

Being as human (at least some of the time) as the next person, I'm not terribly fond of unpleasant circumstances either. I'm not even too fond of the idea of big fish eating little fish, birds eating bugs and worms, big animals preying on smaller ones, and people eating animals. I can choose not to eat animals myself, but there is nothing I know to do to change what goes on in the other kingdoms of Nature. I can't even do very much about immediately changing for the better the circumstances of the world at large—except to live a righteous life, share clear consciousness and assist as opportunities are available to educate and support others who want to be educated and supported. I can also learn to understand why things are as they are, and expand my consciousness until I can clearly comprehend the entire range of cosmic manifestation. In short, I can help to the extent that I can, and I can be anchored in peace of soul in the face of what I cannot immediately help. Please note that I am not denying the existence of challenge in the world. I am simply saying there is a reason for it, because all effects have causes. With understanding, even in the midst of temporary challenge—and all circumstances are temporary—we do not have to suffer.

Circumstances unfold as a result of causes having been put into motion. The effects of causes may be life-disrupting or life-enhancing. There is no denying that most social groups have a percentage of members who are mean-spirited, self-serving and threatening to the order, peace and well-being of the majority. A few members of society are even psychotic, therefore dangerous. Some people may be neurotic, psychotic, or ignorant, but they are not evil. All souls are pure. Ignorance and confusion express as what is termed evil.

There is no evil force or power in contest with God's

But, What About the Evil in the World?

will. Since God is the Oversoul, the cosmic Being, and the universe extends from God, there can be no self-determined evil force or power in the universe. There is no devil, or Satan, except in folklore and myth.

Unable to understand universal processes and the orderly laws of causation, and unwilling to bear personal responsibility for their actions, naive people project their inadequateness upon a nonexistent external cause. The magnitude of social irresponsibility is reflected in a poll taken among members of the general Western population—during which over 50 percent of the people queried admitted to a belief in the devil! Irresponsible people who are too "sophisticated" to believe in the devil may turn elsewhere to place blame—the world's problems are the fault of politicians; there isn't enough money to go around because a few people are greedy; the reason I am lonely is because other people don't know how to demonstrate love; I am not making progress on the spiritual path because of my bad karma; I'm incapable of living a normal life because I grew up in a dysfunctional family—and so on.

Vedic seers referred to the influences in Nature which contribute to illusory perceptions as *maya* (those influences which measure out and provide the basis for objective universal manifestation; cosmic forces and their manifesting subatomic particles, time, space and the causative creative force from which they arise). Man identified with this fabric of Nature, being somewhat deluded, is unable to comprehend its reality. It therefore seems to be in opposition to man's aspirations. New Testament prophets referred to it as Satan (in Hebrew, "the adversary"). The Greek Testament uses as an equivalent *diabolos* ("devil"). In religious language over the centuries these terms were personalized, hence the widespread erroneous acceptance of the devil as a real force in the world. Another common, simplistic teaching is that it is the function of the devil to tempt man away from God.

But what about seemingly otherwise knowledgeable "authorities" who say the devil is real and that an evil power exists? If they affirm it, they are mistaken. Actions and circumstances are commonly referred to as being evil if they interfere with desired unfoldments and spiritual growth. On the other hand, some unpleasant circumstances can contribute to our awakening and to consequent useful changes if our response to them is constructive. A supercilious "everything works out for the best" attitude, about misfortune, is unbecoming of us as beings with potential for rationality. Everything does not always work out for the best. Some circumstances are extremely painful and even spiritually challenging. If we have self-limiting beliefs, we will have to be willing to change our way of looking at life and our way of thinking about God in relation to circumstances if we are to learn to function with mature understanding. We will have to remove ourselves from what is too often considered normal awareness and awaken to a supernatural level of understanding and function.

Supernatural is that which is above and beyond the objective order. When our view of the world is entirely objective, we observe circumstances without acknowledging the inner, subjective side of life. Yet it is the subjective side of Nature which is the realm of inner causes of outer effects. To remove ourselves from attitudes and behaviors which are not useful to higher purposes may require volitional determination, an exercise of conscious choice. A helpful adjunct to doing this, is to accept as our guiding ideal the motto *vitam impendere vero* (Latin, "to consecrate [our] life to truth"). And not only to the apprehension, the understanding, of life's processes but the application of what we learn so that knowledge is demonstrated in our personal circumstances.

How to Pray, with Results Following

Genuine spiritual awareness enables us to intellectually and intuitively determine what is valid or true about God, life processes, soul purpose and how to live our lives. Then by applying what we know, by actualizing or expressing in fact our understanding, fulfillment is assured. Knowing about life is not the same as experiencing life. Obscure or incomplete knowledge will not suffice for our personal purposes or for life's purposes. And knowledge is obscure or incomplete if it is not actualized, because to "know the truth" is to have all darkness dispelled from the mind. When darkness (heaviness, confusion, unknowingness) is absent, the light of perfect understanding prevails. The expression of this understanding then follows naturally and spontaneously.

The "way of the world" is the way of conditioned mental processes and clouded consciousness. The way of knowledge is the way of understanding. The former is the way of complacency or struggle, the latter is the way of relative ease and progressive revelation. Enlightened teachers through the Ages have extended the invitation to "learn what I have learned and be free as I am free." Many reject it. Some are challenged. A few are attracted by the promise but are unable or unwilling to accept the discipline required. A minority hear, respond, apply themselves with diligence and awaken from their dream of mortality to become other than "the race of (mortal) men who walk upon the earth."

When stable in higher knowledge, we should have our needs met effortlessly and be able to accomplish any worthy purpose with relative ease. We should be able to share our understanding with others, heal the sick at heart, cleanse disease from minds and bodies, raise "the living dead" from their unconscious condition, and cast out all confusion and discord from a troubled environment. Nothing spiritually useful should be impossible for us to accomplish. We should have clear memory of our personal history, perfect knowledge of God and cosmic processes and precognitive knowledge of the future. We should thrive, flourish and be successful in all righteous ways. We should be able to control the elements of Nature by soul-inspired intention, when intuitively led to do so.

There should be no unanswered righteous prayers. If our prayers are unanswered it is because we have not prayed correctly; we have either not prayed from a consciousness of divine rapport and soul conviction or we have prayed for effects incompatible with laws natural and supernatural.

It is usually easier to pray successfully for ourselves, because we know our own needs and are better able to know how to help ourselves. When praying for others, results are more likely to be positive if the person prayed for has requested our prayer support and has faith in the process. Even if the person prayed for has no faith, if we pray correctly results will be evident. The most effective way to pray, for ourselves or others, is to first be as God conscious as possible and then see the "nothingness" of the problem or obstacle—seeing and knowing only perfect fulfillment. So when praying for another, we are praying to clear our own understanding which we then share with the person with whom we are working. If we are God conscious when we pray, the person with whom we are working must be included in our God conscious awareness. When God consciousness prevails, causes supporting unwanted circumstances are either dissolved or transcended.

If we have prayed correctly and circumstances do not change for the person prayed with, it may be that conditions about which we have no knowledge are working within the person to assist him in the direction of learning and growth. Also, not all who request prayer support really want to experience change. At a deeper level they may prefer conditions they consciously affirm they would like to have changed. They may not want to undergo psychological and spiritual growth, they may be uncertain about what change will bring, they may not want to disappoint their peers (friends, family members) who have their own expectations and opinions which are supportive of the problem.

It is known that some sick patients, for instance, want their physician to heal them but are unwilling to help themselves. One physician, who is celebrated for his success in assisting seriously ill patients recover, has stated that one of his personal challenges is handling his own feelings because in his experience only about 25 percent of new patients, all with life-threatening illnesses, when offered the choice of helping themselves refuse his recommended program. They are not willing to enter into a regimen of self-examination, psychological growth, and changes in lifestyle which have been proven to be helpful. It is also common that some patients sincerely want to help themselves but allow their friends to poison their minds and dim their hopes by the negative comments they make. Many people whose circumstances are unfortunate, are so dependent that they persist in behaviors which support their circumstances because they then remain unique (the center of attention with their needs provided for by others).

When praying with others, it is all right to pray for specific results but is often more useful to pray that God's will be done. Remember, God's will, the trend of evolution, is growth and fulfillment. When we pray for this, when we know and see only this, we have done our part in the prayer process to remove from the scene any barriers to the free expression of life-transforming influences. Then having done all that is possible, we should retain this consciousness and realization after the prayer interlude. This is what it means to have faith.

It is impossible to have faith without results. To have faith is "to see with clear inner vision all things possible." Faith is influential, it causes change and reproduces itself in the objective world. In *The Gospel According to Saint*

Matthew, an incident is related about the inability of the disciples of Jesus to successfully heal a sick child, which Jesus afterwards did by a simple command. The disciples asked why they were not able to do it, to which Jesus responded (17:29): "Because of your unbelief: for truly I say to you, if you have faith as of a grain of mustard seed, you can say to a mountain, 'Be removed to that place over there,' and it shall be removed; and nothing will be impossible to you." Any circumstance (mountain) can be removed by pure faith. Mustard seed faith is not small faith: it is pure faith. A seed grows into a plant according to its nature. Likewise, needed changes in our lives unfold according to inner conviction and realization. Quiet certainty and clear intention is all that is required. Settled faith is not influenced by mood swings or mental restlessness. The operational modes by which faith results in expression are set into motion by the impulse of our gentle intention and flow without disturbance as we are surrendered to the desired outcome. This is why "praying in secret" is more effective then overt demonstrations of supplication. In surrendered prayer our will is aligned with divine will. We are then not asking the impossible, we are acknowledging the possible with perfect equanimity, perfect self-possessed composure.

What Happens When We Die to this World?

We experience birth so that we do not have to be born again. We experience death so that we do not have to die again. From an absolute perspective we are not really born, nor do we die; we only experience episodes of coming into, and departing relationships and circumstances.

The two most dramatic episodes related to the Earth-experience of most people are birth and death. We are usually somewhat aware of the circumstances of our present incarnation because of recent-memory and present perceptions, but we are not usually as knowledgeable about circumstances prior to physical birth or about what our future after this incarnation will be. The radical shift of consciousness experienced during the birth process (and the sometimes though not always, trauma) suppresses memory of the past. Adaptation to the realm of grosser matter, acceptance of new conditions as being real, and acquired attitudes and behaviors as a result of association with parents and family members can further narrow our focus of perception. The limitations of the body can also restrict our consciousness, because of our identification with it and because of the brain and nervous system being undeveloped during our early years. Constrained by circumstances (the need for physical, emotional and mental development to occur, as well as societal influences), we are not always fortunate enough to know or experience the unfoldment of our soul destiny during our early years on Earth.

Physical birth is a continuation, not the beginning, of our sojourn through space-time. Our origins are in deep, inner space, in the field of pure consciousness. When our reasons for being involved with relative spheres are fulfilled, we will consciously rest in the field of pure consciousness. How did we get involved with the field of matter in the first place? The explanation is simple: as specialized units of consciousness we came into involvement with the flow of creative force from the Godhead as the universe was manifested. We can even say that we are here because of God's will, God's inclination to express. Because of our identification with cosmic mind and matter, we experienced degrees of unconsciousness and forgot our origins and our essential beingness. Identified with mental transformations, moods and relationships, we became temporary citizens of the universe and in this world, assumed the human condition. With awareness diminished and perceptions bounded, the omnipresent soul is thus reduced to the frustration and humiliation of the conditioned-condition. But this is temporary, for at our inmost center of being we really know who and what we are and what our ultimate end will be.

Many souls, despite the restrictions of mind and environment, are aware from the beginning of human experience of an inner brightness, an almost clear knowing of their essence and beingness and an awareness of the dream-like character of the universe which floats in cosmic mind. Many people, as they adapt to this-world circumstances, forget their early perceptions of Reality. Others remain somewhat aware of higher realities but are not impelled to improve upon their partial knowing. A few consciously and intentionally commit themselves to study and learning, and to further actualizing their divine attributes and capacities. They become disciples on an enlightenment path.

Most of us have been on Earth before. We always move toward, and attract, circumstances and relationships which are compatible with our states of consciousness and mental states. If we do not know how to remove ourselves (or do not want to) from conditions as we know them, we tend to maintain them. If we have reasons for experiencing conditions and relationships, we seek them out. Thus reincarnation is, for most souls, a necessity. For souls with purpose, who have unfinished business or who are playing a role in the unfolding evolutionary drama, reincarnation is an opportunity.

Many who easily accept the fact of reincarnation have questions about the process. How long will they continue to reincarnate? What happens to souls between Earth-life episodes? And with the present global human population approaching 6-billion, as compared to the relatively small populations of past millennia, where are all the souls coming from? There are other questions: Do we meet again in this and other realms? Do we experience gender changes between incarnations? What happens to people who commit suicide? Why are some people born dysfunctional?

We continue to experience cycles of return until we

What Happens When We Die to this World?

outgrow the necessity for doing so, or until our desires and purposes have been fulfilled. Between physical embodiments we experience life in subtle astral and causal spheres. Multiplied trillions of souls inhabit the universe (and possibly other universes) in physical, astral and causal realms. Their flowing between spheres is constant. We do not know how many human beings have preceded us on Planet Earth. Human beings have been here for at least 100,000 years, perhaps longer, and human types have been here for at least a million years. Souls may also flow through the animal kingdoms, so it is believed by some, until they awaken to levels where a human form is needed for continued growth. Souls also continually flow from the field of God and from manifest fields to God. We meet again and again if we have enough in common to allow for a relationship. Gender changes between incarnations are not an impossibility, but they are not a necessity. People who commit suicide, victims of abortion or interrupted pregnancies, and those who experience transition by violent means continue their experiences according to their states of consciousness and mental states. Parenthood should be planned and the responsibilities that go along with it voluntarily assumed. Wanton performance of abortion is an irresponsible and violent act. The occasion for deciding against pregnancy is before conception and violence of any kind is contrary to our highest philosophical, moral and spiritual principles.

Human life should ordinarily be long and healthy. Our learning opportunities are just as available in this world as in any other and if we learn our lessons well, we do not have to involuntarily return. We may return by choice, to satisfy curiosity or to serve the cause of evolution. Thankfully, regardless of the varied conditions prevailing on the world scene, there are always many conscious souls embodied so that knowledge is never absent from the world. The presence of such souls is essential for the elevation of the human race and for the continued transformation of planetary consciousness.

When the occasion for the transition is near, one

should withdraw attention from outer involvements and go more deeply into soul consciousness. This frequently happens naturally, as psychological adjustments occur and transcendent insights coincide with an increasing disinterest in world affairs. The most valuable training for eventual transition is meditation. When we meditate, we die to the world. Having learned to do this consciously, fear of death and after death states dissolves. As a result, our outlook on life changes. We can enjoy relationships and activities, we can satisfy our curiosity, we can enthusiastically perform our duties, while knowing that we are participants in the drama of life and that the best of all possible ways to play our role is to do so with surrendered compliance with all that is highest and best, for ourselves and others.

While the transition process has been known to members of mystical and esoteric groups for centuries, it is but recently that information has become more widely published. One reason for this is that more people are openly sharing their experiences about their own near-death episodes. Hundreds of stories have been collected during the past decade, most of them bearing striking similarities.

Individuals involved in serious accidents, or whose vital signs have ceased to be apparent while under the supervision of a physician or being cared for by others, have told of being out of the body—hovering over the body or standing off to one side yet still conscious and perceptive. Many have told of inner journeys "through a tunnel of light" and emerging into a luminous sphere inhabited by "wise beings" and/or friends and relatives who had died earlier. For the most part, such experiences have been extremely pleasant, even ecstatic, sometimes so intensely satisfying that return to body consciousness was no longer desirable. Frequently, during the episode the person would be told that it was not yet time for final transition, that a return to Earth-life duties and opportunities must be accepted. Many reported extreme reluctance in having to withdraw from what was perceived as a heaven-like condition. Almost without exception, their lives were dramatically altered. They did not fear death, they were more content with their relationships and learning opportunities and they were kinder and more caring about others and the planet. It seemed that they had been given a preview of next-world conditions and their consciousness remained permanently changed for the better as a result.

There are instances of near-death experiences being confusing, but these are rare. Just as it is natural to be born into the world, when conditions are right it is just as natural to leave it. And just as there are some souls which come into the world with psychological conflicts, there are some who depart with similar problems. The fewer the psychological conflicts and the more complete is emotional growth, the easier it is to experience birth and transition without uneasiness or trauma.

The experiences shared by persons who have undergone near-death episodes are similar to those reported by some meditators. I am not suggesting that one need to be wary of meditating or that one attempt while meditating to have such experiences, only that they have been known to occur. When they occur spontaneously they are pleasant and educational. Advanced meditators often focus attention at the spiritual eye, the point between the eyebrows, when meditating. When deep relaxation occurs and life forces are withdrawn from the body's extremities and flow steadily into the spiritual eye, a light is perceived. Initially, this light is a manifestation of vital forces converging at the medulla of the brain and reflecting in the spiritual eye. A tunnel of light may be perceived and the meditator feels as though he is being drawn through this tunnel, sometimes with great speed. Emerging from the tunnel of light one's awareness blends with a sphere of brilliant light, sometimes with perceptions of "benevolent beings" present and sometimes by a knowing that this is the beginning of an inner journey to higher levels of perception.

When approaching the occasion of final transition a

meditator can surrender to the process and because of prior meditation experiences, move through illusory perceptions projected into the mind by emotional unrest and mental transformations, to clear astral or causal realms or beyond them to conscious transcendence of all relative phenomena.

When a person departs this world it is usually the close friends and associates who remain here who have problems coming to terms with the event; the departed soul is continuing its journey to ultimate fulfillment. Because of our body-centered focus we often rejoice at the birth of a child and resent the intrusion of physical death. When reminded of our physical mortality we are often depressed. But every birth is followed by physical death, and every physical death is followed by birth into another sphere of expression. This is how the life process is, and we can learn to understand and cooperate with it.

The only things that will heal grief and emotional unrest when someone we love leaves a relationship are time and understanding. If understanding is clear, loss may be felt but will more easily be handled. It is always useful to come to terms with the event and rest in the conviction that since life supports us, life is also continuing to support the person who is no longer with us. As you pray for yourself and for others in this world, pray also for the welfare of those in other spheres. It is generally not recommended that we attempt to establish telepathic communication with souls which have passed on. Spontaneous occasions of communication are known: as a clear awareness of a presence, a vision, or in a lucid dream. Spiritually advanced persons report such incidents as being natural to their experience. Persons not so spiritually advanced, while at times having such experiences, may also be likely to hallucinate or unconsciously create wish-fulfilling incidents of seeming-communication as a way to pacify their minds. The three obviously expressing spheres most easily accessible to souls relating to Earth are the physical realm in which we currently reside, the astral realm of life forces, and the causal realm of fine aura-electricities which support astral and physical realms. After transition one may experience a consciousness-shift to astral experience. Here, one may experience an environment much like the Earth realm in appearance. Some astral spheres are more ethereal and some are heaven-like. In causal spheres the soul is devoid of an astral sheath (body) and moves through causal spaces by intention, shifting viewpoints at will. When weary of astral or causal experiences one may be inspired to transcend them and become more consciously aware of the field of God, or to return to involvement with sensory experiences—resulting in continued dwelling in astral or causal spheres, or in physical rebirth. The governing principle is that one tends to relate to an environment which is compatible with states of consciousness and personal desires.

It is a mistake to assume that spiritual growth will be easier in realms other than where we are. In astral and causal realms, one is not as restricted as one might be when expressing through a physical body, but if psychological conflicts remain and if higher understanding is not unfolded, other-realm environments are not necessarily more supportive. It is far better to choose to live the present life-cycle well and to facilitate spiritual growth while the opportunity to do so is at hand. Similarly, to conclude that the reasonable thing to do, if spiritual growth is not presently satisfactory, is to "wait until the next incarnation when circumstances might be better," is a drastic mistake. We are already living in eternity—in the field of endless time. Instead of wondering, as some people do, how you will experience eternity, ask yourself, "How am I living in eternity, now?" Where we are and what we are doing, is how we are living in eternity. Ask yourself, "What am I in this world to do?" Find out what you are here to do, and do it.

The Seven Levels of Soul Awareness that Determine Perception, Behavior and Experience

How long have you been consciously on a spiritual growth path? And what have been your discoveries? How much time, effort and thought have you given to the process—and what have been your results?

We can fairly easily determine our present level of awareness and understanding by how we function: by how we think, feel and behave. While every soul is a specialized unit of pure consciousness, when souls are identified with mental conditions and awareness is filtered through them, varied levels of awareness express. The following seven categories are recognized in varying degrees in the general population. While some characteristics of other levels may be expressive at any time, a dominant level will be most obviously determining of ability to function. Several esoteric traditions relate levels of soul awareness to the chakras, the centers along the spinal pathway and in the brain through which consciousness expresses.

1. *Unconscious* – While somewhat conscious and functional, at this level one is inclined to be identified with the senses and the objective world. Because of this there is little awareness of soul capacities or of higher potential. Understanding of life processes and the real nature of God is difficult. If religious, one may identify with a traditional belief system but not be inclined to grow in understanding. Death may be thought of as final, with perhaps a hope of future resurrection. Persons at this level of awareness who believe in reincarnation will tend to think in terms of endless rounds of Earth experience. Chakra level: base of spine.

2. *Subconscious* – While more conscious and func-

The Seven Levels of Soul Awareness

tional, at this level one is usually strongly influenced by subconscious tendencies and mental conditionings and is dominated by emotions. Because of this, misperception is common, resulting in illusions, confusion and doubts about the purpose and meaning of life. One at this level may be overly dependent upon relationships or addicted to self-limiting behaviors. If religious, or inclined to discover ways to facilitate spiritual growth, one may be attracted to possibilities of religious experiences of an emotionally satisfying nature, or if more inclined to esoteric studies may desire visions, ecstatic experiences or involvement with astral perceptions. A large number of "new age" participants are functioning from this level (and the one described next). Chakra level: sacrum.

3. *Self-conscious* – At this level one is more awake but is still strongly influenced by mental transformations, self-centeredness (egoism) and the consequent need to be in control. One at this level may have aspirations for spiritual growth and is usually efficient in the use of imagination and executive abilities; that is, one is able to be self-determined and self-responsible for relationships and actions. If strongly self-centered, creative abilities will be used selfishly. If more spiritually awakened, abilities will be used unselfishly. If religious, one's religion must be meaningful, it must be practical. If inclined to facilitate psychological and spiritual growth, one will choose a reasonable path and be results-oriented. Many people at this level enjoy meditation for the immediate personal benefits: stress reduction, improved function, mental clarity, increased energy, and to contribute to total wellness. Chakra level: lumbar.

4. *Superconscious* – At this level one is more knowledgeable about spiritual realities and finds it easy to accept that, as souls, everyone is "made in the image and likeness of God." The inclination is to be selfless, to know life's purpose and to cooperate with it. Meditation is easy, natural and spontaneous, with subtle and fine perceptions and occasions of cosmic awareness, God awareness and pure consciousness. Subconscious influences are less

dominant and behavior tends to be entirely life-enhancing. If religious, one will be inclined to an intentional path of discipleship in order to experience rapid spiritual growth. Chakra level: dorsal.

5. *Cosmic Conscious* – At this level one has frequent perceptions (and knowledge) of the universe as a play of cosmic forces and increasing perceptions of the reality of God, along with experiences of God consciousness. One will be focused, purposeful and spontaneously responsive to evolutionary forces contributing to steady spiritual growth. One is spontaneously "good" and lives a pure, simple life while creatively involved with worthy purposes. Chakra level: cervical.

6. *God Conscious* – At this level one has understanding of the nature of God and conscious experience of God as the pervading reality in, through, and as everything. From cosmic conscious levels partial perceptions of God unfold, then blossom into full realization. Chakra level: spiritual eye.

7. *Enlightened* – Complete realization of the soul as a specialized unit of pure consciousness, complete knowledge and experience of God and complete awareness of the field of pure consciousness beyond form and attributes. While embodied, one has complete understanding of the operations of cosmic forces in all spheres and at all levels of manifestation. Enlightenment is complete soul liberation. Chakra level: crown.

We contribute to our psychological and spiritual growth when we provide for ourselves supportive circumstances in which life can fulfill its purposes. Since consciousness expresses through mind and body, the more responsive the mind, brain, nervous system and body are, the more easily does consciousness express. This is why, at all levels of awareness it is useful to cooperate with Nature's laws, choose a pure food diet, ensure a personal environment which is pollution-free*, choose behaviors which are

* I refer here not only to obvious physical surroundings, but also to being removed from sources of magnetic fields emitted by electric power lines

supportive of relationships, live a purposeful life attending to all duties in a cheerful manner, and to engage in regular spiritual practices for the purpose of expanding awareness and contributing to psychological transformation and the refinement of the brain and nervous system.

Surrendered aspiration to grow spiritually, as well as regular superconscious episodes experienced during the practice of contemplative meditation, result in superconscious states which powerfully, beneficially influence the brain and nervous system. As the brain and nervous system become more refined, consciousness is more easily processed in the body, enabling us to experience and maintain higher states of consciousness with relative ease. There are centers in the brain and body where consciousness connects and through which it flows. When these centers are cleared, consciousness expresses spontaneously and wellness is manifested and maintained.

At progressive growth-stages there may be occasions of uncertainty because of shifts of consciousness. The occasions are not unlike the stages through which we move from childhood to adolescence, and from early adulthood through the later stages of psychological growth. As the ego becomes less pronounced and awareness expands, our understanding improves and some of our priorities change. This may require an evaluation of lifestyle, relationships and behavior. One may say, "I'm not the same person I used to be, but I'm not yet the person I know I will be." During these phases, keep on with worthwhile practices and routines while being open to guidance and understanding. These transitional phases are nothing to be unduly concerned about and will be transcended. At these times it may be useful to go on a spiritual retreat, to get away from environmental conditions which may be

---

and electrical appliances, as well as being removed from sources of possible mental and emotional contamination. The latter is assured by choosing relationships and by learning to be impervious to negative conversations, attitudes and behaviors of others with whom necessity requires a relationship.

difficult to deal with and to go more deeply into spiritual awareness. Also, avoid worry, anxiety and the inclination to discuss your challenges with friends who do not understand what you are going through. The advice of a spiritually aware friend, or spiritual teacher, could be helpful, as can reading inspirational books and intentional planning sessions. By maintaining a positive mental attitude, exercising patience and being open to grace, necessary adjustments will occur within you and around you. It will also be necessary to take what seems to be correct steps, to encourage the actualization of higher levels of consciousness. In other words, start doing what needs to be done to move into, and be grounded in the next level of awareness and function.

Righteousness and Grace:
Learning to Let God Do It

We want to live a righteous life, in harmony with God's will and the supportive laws of Nature, and we want to experience elevations of consciousness which will enable us to be removed from self-centered behavior and open to grace—but we do not always know how to align ourselves with elemental cosmic forces or trust in the kindly purposes of evolutionary influences. We are often at the juncture of being inclined to hold on to the old ways while, at the same time, wanting to let go and allow ourselves opportunities to test whether or not the universe will meet our needs. This continuing challenge is due to the fact that awakening man, unfolding from sense-bound material consciousness to soul and God consciousness, is sooner or later forced by the very process of growth to learn new ways of viewing his world and new ways of relating to it.

Thankfully, there is a higher, more fulfilling way to satisfy our needs and accomplish our purposes than to struggle at a level of conditioned behavior. In *The Gospel*

According to Saint Matthew (6:19-34) the issue is addressed. (I have paraphrased the verses, using common English for clarification.)

> Lay not up for yourselves treasures in this world, where they can be corrupted or taken from you. But lay up for yourselves treasures in heaven (your consciousness of higher realization) where they are removed from the possibility of corruption or loss. For where your treasure is, there will be your true concern also. The light of the body is in the eye: if your vision is focused on what is important, your whole life will be full of light. No man can serve two masters: for either he will hate the one, and love the other; or be attached to the one, and despise the other. You cannot serve God (the natural order) and at the same time be attached to externals. Therefore I say to you, take no anxious thought for your life, about what you shall have to eat, or what you shall have to drink; and do not be anxiously concerned for your body, what you shall wear. Is not life more than food, and is not the body more than the clothes you wear? Behold the birds of the air: for they sow not, neither do they reap, nor hoard food; yet Nature provides for them. Are you not much better than they? And which of you by thinking can cause your body to grow taller? Why then are you overly concerned about clothing? Consider the flowers in the field, how they grow; they do not work hard. And yet I say to you that even Solomon in all his glory was not arrayed like one of these. So if God (as Nature) provides for the grass of the field, which like you is subject to being here for a duration and then dying, shall he not even more provide for you, you of little faith? Therefore take no anxious thought, saying such things as, "What shall we eat? or, what shall we drink? or how will we be clothed?" For after all these things do self-centered people seek. God knows you have need of these things. But seek first the knowledge of God and a relationship with God, and be in harmony with the processes of life both natural and divine; and all these things will be provided you. Take no anxious thought about the future, for the future will be taken care of. To

be overly anxious about day-to-day matters is a limitation that restricts the flow of grace.

The King James version (6:33) reads: "But seek ye first the kingdom of God, and his righteousness; and all these things shall be added unto you." The *kingdom of God* is the level of conscious understanding at which knowledge of God and life processes is present. God's righteousness is the orderly process of unfoldment; therefore, when we are sufficiently spiritually aware and in harmony with "the way of righteousness," everything in our lives effortlessly flows in divine order.

What causes this effortless flow is grace, the creative impulse with origins in God, the Oversoul, and which extends throughout all of creation to contribute to orderly fulfillment of purposes. It contributes to the orderly fulfillment of higher purposes of which we are not always aware. Because grace cannot be manipulated by us—but only accepted—it is referred to as a gift of God.

There is no need for us to question whether or not we are worthy of grace; that is, whether or not we deserve it because of our attitudes and behavior. We need not even ponder the matter of whether or not God can withhold grace, for God cannot. It is the nature of grace to flow through avenues open to it. The effects of grace are healing, redemptive, cleansing and illuminating. Grace contributes to spiritual growth, mental acuity, psychological wellness, physical function, supportive relationships, orderly unfoldment of circumstances, a sufficiency of all needed things, and the eventual fulfillment of soul destiny. Grace does what we cannot do and opens doors which cannot be unlocked by ordinary means.

When we are sincerely seeking higher understanding and are desirous of spiritual growth, are led to help ourselves in constructive ways, and are provided with useful assistance in unplanned ways, this is grace. When we learn how to use our talents and skills to help ourselves in the right way, this is grace. When adjustments in consciousness and in mental attitude suddenly occur and make a real difference in our lives, this is grace. When we acquire useful information about how to contribute to our own wellness and are motivated from within to help ourselves, this is grace. When we are trusting enough to extend ourselves to others and accept their love and support, this is grace. When we assume responsibility for our behavior and focus energies on matters of priority, this is grace. When our needs are met because of personal efforts and in unplanned ways, this is grace. When we are at a crossroads in life and inspiration unfolds to provide us insight, this is grace. When we are faced with an impossible situation and cannot help ourselves, but the situation is resolved harmoniously, this is grace. If we will but review our personal history we will be able to acknowledge occasions beyond numbering when "something" helped us when we could not help ourselves, or help was provided even when we did not know at the time that it was needed. These are episodes of grace. During occasions of secluded contemplation, when we are inwardly examining higher states of consciousness and the possibility of ultimate discovery, the final breakthroughs are the result of grace—because we cannot make them happen, we can only prepare for them.

The currents of evolution (grace) are flowing through the universe with purpose, and transformation and growth are the results of this insistent influence. The way to be more open to the flow of grace is to be responsive to it: by ordering personal affairs, clearing the mind of distractions, attaining a degree of emotional maturity, contributing to the wellness and refinement of the body, and doing our best to ensure that our purposes are in harmony with the trend of evolution. When we are in harmony with the trend of evolution we are in alignment with the way of righteousness. Then whatever we really need is supplied, and whatever we are inspirationally led to do will result in successful outcomes—not only for us but for all whose lives are touched by our own. Grace always blesses.

Learning to be open to grace is learning to let go and let God express. The innate inclination of God, in relationship to the universe, is to fulfill intentional purposes—to move in the direction of growth and completion. *When our purposes are aligned with evolutionary purposes, we are certain to experience their unfoldment along with the fulfillment of life's purposes.* This is the certain way to definitely experience inner peace, spiritual growth and the fulfillment of destiny.

Fate is related to causation. The causes we put into motion because of conscious intentional desires—or because of unconscious inclinations, whims and behaviors—tend to reproduce after themselves. Ego-motivated desires, as well as urges for experience which arise because of internal confusion, bear surface results and can keep us bound to the wheel of causation for countless eons of time. Unless we change our behaviors, or unless grace intervenes (as it often does, and eventually will), we are fated to experience the effects of present internal causes. Many people who are not yet spiritually awake are in reasonable control of their lives and mistakenly believe themselves to be masters of their own destiny. They may be, instead, merely reinforcing behaviors which actually inhibit the actualization of their soul potential. This is not to say that we should not be disciplined, that we should not be intentional, that we should not be as responsible as possible for helping ourselves—we should, but while doing so we should also be open to further spiritual growth, increased understanding and ever alert to signs of God's grace intruding into our affairs. As egoism decreases, grace increases and life's purposes are more easily fulfilled. Fate, then, is related to the causes we put into motion and the influences of circumstances about us which we allow to affect us. Fate has to do with externals, with surface transformations and changes. Destiny is that which cannot ultimately be avoided—and what cannot ultimately be avoided is spiritual growth and illumination of consciousness. We came into involvement with the relative spheres and we will eventually be removed from them. We came from the field of God and we will eventually be restored to God awareness. This cannot be prevented. This is destiny. We can, by unwise or unconscious exercise of will, somewhat resist the trend of destiny, but we cannot forever avoid it. We are wise when we accept what life has planned for us and cooperate with the process. We are foolish when we do not.

One of the most helpful abilities we have is that of envisioning possibilities other than those which presently prevail, which restrict our creative expression and frustrate the soul's inclination to completely awaken and be restored to understanding. We may feel so completely at the mercy of limiting circumstances that we don't know what to do to help ourselves or where to turn for relief. We may be tired and discouraged because of having honestly done our human best, without satisfying results. We may be reasonably comfortable and successful in the eyes of the world, but inwardly unfulfilled because our psychological and spiritual growth has been neglected—or if attended to, is not satisfying.

Well, how would it be for us if there were no limiting circumstances in our lives? How would we feel if we knew there was something to which to turn that could move into our lives with transforming power? What would happen if we were able to see beyond our present condition and be established in the understanding of all things possible? What then? Our states of consciousness would be easily adjusted to a higher level, our mental states would become entirely constructive. Our behaviors would be life-enhancing. Our lifestyle would change to conform with entirely supportive circumstances. Problems would be solved. Confidence would dissolve uncertainty and fear. Internal conflicts would be resolved. Nothing worthy of us would be impossible to actualize. Memories and traumas of the past would no longer influence our moods and behaviors. Anxiety about the future would cease. The prospect of death would be a laughable impossibility.

If we live righteously, if we do what we honestly can to help ourselves, if we attend to spiritual practices, we will steadily grow to maturity. *If we do these things while envisioning all things possible—our lives will be enriched and psychological and spiritual growth more obviously quickened!*

Unless an unexpected shift of consciousness occurs, unless grace intercedes, what our present states of consciousness and mental states are, will continue to determine our concept of ourselves and our pattern of circumstances. If we remain as we are, in consciousness and understanding, circumstances will continue to be perceived and experienced as they presently are. By a conscious and intentional adjustment of attitude, by purposely envisioning more desirable and higher possibilities, our view of the world changes and we open ourselves to life. Creative capacities unfold. Intellectual powers increase. Appreciation for life and its opportunities is enhanced. Energies formerly restrained are released. Intuitional insights provide knowledge. We become happy. Circumstances become harmonious and supportive. Resources are made available to us. Unplanned good fortune is experienced. Righteous behavior is spontaneous. Life-as-it-is is wonderful and the future is glorious.

We are all the same as expressions of the Divine, but you are unique. You are important to the wellness of the world. Consciously acknowledge this, for at the inmost level of your being, you know it. No matter who you are, where you live on Planet Earth, what your background has been, what color your skin is or your cultural origins, what form of worship you choose, what useful lifestyle you have, you are innately good and the world is blessed because of you.

Yes, you are important to the process. Every constructive thought you think, every inspired act you perform, every caring feeling you have, benefits me and everyone else. Beyond this, your silent influence extends to the smallest units of matter and to the most distant galaxy. You do not think a thought or have a feeling, however subtle or obvious, but that the universe is influenced.

When you are happy, the world is happier. When you are healthy, the world is healthier. When you are surrendered in God, the world is more harmonious. Your peace, your understanding, your being, contributes to the peace, understanding and spiritual awareness of all souls in this and, other, worlds.

I could quote a thousand sources to affirm this truth. I would be but echoing what has been said, perhaps better, so many times before: No man is an island; We are all one family; The universe is one organic whole; Not a sparrow falls but that God knows; Wherever and whenever unrighteousness prevails, providence intercedes to set virtue on her seat again.

There will never be another you. Your coming into this world was with purpose. No person has had your thoughts, experienced your feelings, perceived life as you have perceived it or dreamed your dreams. Nothing you have done or will do, has ever been duplicated by another. No person has ever loved as you have loved, or been loved as you have been loved.

From the ocean of life, you came into expression. Your way is personal and when you are conscious of your personal way, your destined way, do not depart from it. It is good to have the acknowledgement of others; it is better to have the inner acknowledgement of the soul which informs you of your right place in the natural order.

If you had not been born into the world, the world would not be exactly as it is, because you have made a difference. You will continue to make a difference as you unfold and grow in righteousness and grace.

THREE

Your Personalized Program

From the beginning until the ending of
  time, there is a love between Thee and
  me: and how shall such love be
  extinguished
Kabir says, "As the river enters into the
  ocean, so my heart touches Thee."
  KABIR (1823-1896)
  Songs

Love God and you will be humble: love God and you will throw off the love of self: love God and you will love all that He gives you to love for love of Him.
  FRANÇOIS FENELON (1651-1715)
  Sermons

We are living in the midst of death. What is the value of working for our own schemes when they might be reduced to naught? But we feel as strong as a rock, if we could truthfully say we work for God and his schemes. Then nothing perishes.
  MOHANDAS K. GANDHI (1869-1948)
  Selected Addresses

When God wanted sponges and oysters, He made them, and put one on a rock, and the other in the mud. When He made man, He did not make him to be a sponge or an oyster; He made him with feet, and hands, and head, and heart, and vital blood, and a place to use them, and said to him, "Go, work!"
  HENRY WARD BEECHER (1813-1887)
  Royal Truths

Your Personalized Program for Definitely Experiencing Inner Peace, Spiritual Growth and the Fulfillment of Life's Purposes

In the preceding chapters we have had an opportunity to examine the principles which, if understood and applied, can contribute to our ability to live with greater ease as well as to our psychological and spiritual growth. Now, we focus on what to do to actually help ourselves become increasingly open to life. Carefully examine what is here recommended and apply yourself with self-honest diligence. Personal application will provide experience and experience will result in knowledge.

The four essentials to the fulfillment of your major purposes in life are:

1. *Personal Perception* – How you see yourself and how you view yourself in relationship to your world, determine your experiences. What seems presently real to you is your perception of reality. This is your *paradigm**, your working concept with which you approach problem-solving, set goals, make decisions and enter into relationships of all kinds. You relate to the world according to how you view yourself in relationship to it, according to your assumptions, beliefs or accurate perceptions. Your conviction of purpose, your attitudes, and behaviors will usually coincide with your prevailing perceptions. If you believe yourself to be a restricted human being, you will think, feel and act accordingly. If you believe life to be hopeless, you will be subject to confusion and despair. If you believe all

---

* *PARE-AH-DIME* (Greek *Paradeigma*, "pattern")

things possible, you will be enthusiastic and keenly interested in relationships and life processes. If your present view of yourself and the world is one of limitation, positive thinking and intentional efforts to help yourself *can* be useful, but belief in limitations may restrict successful outcomes. Such efforts may result in attempts to cope rather than to excel, to attempt rather than to accomplish, to struggle rather than to spontaneously and joyfully express. If you can understand that you are a spiritual being living in a spiritual universe and that your relationship with God is already a fact, you will be able to more easily put aside concepts, attitudes, behaviors and relationships which are not useful to your higher purposes.

2. *Attitude* – Your outlook on life constitutes your mental attitude. If based on understanding, it reveals your soul vision; what you know to be true, rather than upon illusory perceptions. Can you see all things possible? Your perception of yourself and your world determines your attitude.

3. *Purpose* – Your perceptions and your attitude determine your sense (or knowledge of) purposes. How big are you? How big is your world? Why are you here? What are you to do? What are you now doing, or willing to do, to experience your worthy purposes and to allow life's purposes to be fulfilled through and, around, you? If you are *on purpose*, you will be disciplined enough, emotionally mature enough, to eliminate nonessentials and focus on important relationships and behaviors in order to accomplish your purposes as efficiently as possible. Are you doing this?

4. *Behavior* – Your perception of yourself and your world, your attitude, and your sense of purpose, determine your behavior, and your behavior unfailingly reveals what your mental states and states of consciousness are. Ideal behavior (right behavior) is based on understanding. Even with a degree of inner understanding, if you are not purposeful, if you do not do what you need to do, there will be few satisfactory outcomes. However, even if you are not capable of performing from an optimum level, if you can

mentally envision desired outcomes, they will unfold, resulting in psychological adjustments and spiritual growth. You do not have to be spiritually advanced to behave appropriately; you have only to be willing to do necessary things as duty, as being appropriate. In this way you train yourself to do your responsible best, contribute to your emotional maturity and open yourself to spiritual growth possibilities.

Remember, as you proceed, that true soul contentment is not the effect of outer accomplishment. You may, by diligent self-effort, "gain the whole world" and still be lacking in peace of soul. Permanent spiritual joy will be experienced when you are settled in soul awareness and firm in your clear understanding of your relationship with God. From this basis you can attend to your duties, enjoy meaningful relationships and fulfill your purposes correctly.

The best way to achieve goals is to learn how to proceed, without anxiety, egoism or emotional attachment to end results. This is the way of effortless-effort, the way of doing-without-striving, the way of accomplishment-without-grasping. Live because living is enjoyable. Accomplish because there are necessary and meaningful things to do. Have fun. Train yourself to live well, without being overly proud of your accomplishments and without being disappointed when things don't always work out exactly as you had planned. Leave space in your life for unplanned good fortune, for the working out of a higher law than your personal contrivances. In this way you will be functional, productive, successful and in the flow of life's goodness, and you will avoid egotism as a result of success and pain as a result of thwarted expectations. Transcend pride and the need to dominate circumstances, and you will be happier and healthier in all ways.

Remember the four primary aims of life (to live with purpose and attend to personal duties; to have legitimate needs satisfied; to be in harmony with the universe in order to be nourished by it and to be supplied with resources with which to accomplish worthy purposes; to experience progressive spiritual growth and experience God-realization) and include them all in a balanced living program. To neglect any one of these, is to live an imbalanced and incomplete life.

Consciously Choose a Lifestyle
Fully Supportive of Your Worthy
Purposes and Spiritual Growth

We are not in this world to glorify ourselves. We are here to learn to allow God to be glorified through and around us. What can we do to contribute to this process? We can learn how to live, and surrender to the processes.

All that is required is reasonable understanding and willingness to apply what is learned. From this, wisdom blossoms, along with the many gifts of life. And life's unfoldments are gifts: they are free and accessible because life is one self-manifesting, complete within itself, expression of Divine intention. We are specialized expressions of life, participating in the unfolding drama we perceive and experience. Therefore, when we are cooperatively surrendered, we naturally play our proper roles and fulfill life's purposes with the full support of the universe. With understanding, and surrendered participation, we become wise in the ways of the world and wise in the ways of God. We learn life's processes and we discover inner causes of outer effects.

If your present lifestyle does not fully support your higher aspirations, including psychological and spiritual growth, then make necessary adjustments so that your lifestyle is fully supportive. You cannot become what you deserve to be, by remaining as you are. You cannot demonstrate intelligence, or implement useful changes, by behaving unreasonably or remaining attached to relationships and circumstances which are not life-enhancing. So begin where you are, with what you have to work with, and put as much order in your personal environment as possible. Eliminate *everything* that is not supportive, that is not elevating and constructive. Live simply, with understanding intention. Be focused. Know your purposes and be on purpose. Don't be a slave to possessions or environmental circumstances. Be self (soul) directed, instead of allowing your life to be determined by whims, moods, the opinions of others, and by unnecessary involvements and activities. Bless yourself and others by your cheerful, positive presence and behavior. Avoid allowing the dependency needs of emotionally unstable people to influence your lifestyle.

Be self-responsible for your psychological maturity, physical wellness, supportive relationships, and the performance of your duties. Take to heart the words of Emerson*: "It is easy to live after the world's opinions; it is easy in solitude to live after our own; but the great man is he who in the midst of the crowd keeps with perfect sweetness the independence of solitude." Enjoy relationships, enjoy living, but without attachments and without being wrongly influenced.

Live to give, not to get. Out of the depthless ocean of formless life, all forms emerge. From within us, because we are grounded in the boundless field of Existence, all knowledge, all understanding, all happiness and joy emerge. God has already provided us everything because the universe is God-manifesting and expressing. Knowing this, we can learn to participate with universal creative processes and share what we are, and what we have, with others.

Cultivate the virtues and live in harmony with the rhythms of the universe. The guidelines have been given us by various teachers through the Ages and they apply for all people, of all times. Buddhism, as an example, teaches "the middle path" and "the eightfold path." The middle path is "that path which opens the eyes and bestows

---

* Essay, *Self-Reliance*, Ralph Waldo Emerson (1803-1882)

understanding, which leads to peace of mind, to the higher wisdom, to full enlightenment, to nirvana (transcendence)." The eightfold path is the way of "right view (perception and attitude), right aspiration, right speech, right conduct right livelihood, right effort, right mindfulness (seeing clearly), and right contemplation."

Your present choice of lifestyle reflects your states of consciousness and mental states, and your opinion of yourself. If your present lifestyle is fully supportive of your highest aspirations, nurture it. If your present lifestyle is not fully supportive of your highest aspirations, change it. Where and how you choose to live, what you choose to do with your time and energy, your vocation or occupation, your choice of friends—everything you do, and allow, is your personal choice. If you feel improvements are in order but do not know how to make improvements, or if you feel circumstances are restrictive but do not know how to heal or change circumstances, carefully attend to the recommended procedures which follow.

Meditate for Personal Benefits and Accelerated Spiritual Growth

The foundation practice which ensures inner peace and opens our consciousness to the Infinite, is meditation. Meditation is not only for persons on an intentional spiritual growth path, it is today being practiced on a regular schedule by thousands of people in all walks of life who enjoy the life-enhancing benefits which result from correct, regular practice.

Meditation, correctly and regularly practiced, contributes to stress reduction, orderly thinking, improved intellectual capacities, constructive mental states, balancing of the body's vital forces and strengthening of its immune system. Meditation also slows biological aging processes. Meditators tend to be health-minded, more disease resistant and creatively functional.

Superconscious meditation should not be confused with self-hypnosis or other mind-conditioning procedures. Superconsciousness is a level of awareness which is quite apart from the usually influential unconscious, subconscious, and ordinary waking states. During superconsciousness the mental modifications (thought transformations, illusions due to misperception, hallucinations, and sleep conditions) are transcended; that is, attention is removed from them. Superconscious meditation allows us the opportunity to experience deep rest and to explore subtle and fine levels of awareness.

During superconscious meditation, and afterwards when meditative calm persists, superior influential forces flow through the mental field, nervous system and body, to contribute to balancing and ordering the systems. Destructive mental and emotional tendencies are resisted, weakened, and dissolved by superconscious influences, resulting in heightened awareness and improved function. This is why meditation practice contributes to the acceleration, the quickening, of spiritual evolution.

Meditation should be practiced at the same time every day, if possible. Meditate consciously and correctly, and sit long enough to experience deep relaxation and serenity. In this way, every session will be productive and you will soon notice that you not only enjoy your interlude of meditative quiet; you also begin to anticipate the opportunity to meditate when it is once again time to sit in the silence.

Some people find meditation easy to experience, and they are able to immediately surrender to the process as it unfolds naturally and spontaneously. Others, however, report that mental restlessness, emotional unrest, and stress interfere with their attempts to concentrate effectively. It is for this purpose that specific psycho-physiological meditation techniques are recommended. They enable the meditator to do certain things to contribute to relaxation and easy concentration, without extreme effort and with pleasant results.

The mind has an innate pleasure-grasping inclination. This has survival and goal-achievement value, because a degree of pleasure or satisfaction is experienced when we do things which contribute to personal survival and the accomplishment of purposes. Eating, breathing, recreation, sleep, exercise, emotional satisfaction derived from comfortable relationships, fulfillment of desire—all result in feelings of pleasure and mental satisfaction. However, if the senses are not regulated, if desires are not wisely monitored, the desire of the mind to be restored to peace can result in behavior which is sometimes obsessive and not always constructive. We see this demonstrated by many people whose lives are determined by a frantic quest for happiness, or who indulge in behaviors and relationships which afford a degree of comfort but which are, in the long run, not useful to higher purposes. This can result in addictive, self-limiting preoccupations.

But we can utilize the mind's innate inclination to be satisfied by introducing the mind to the superior, more refined, and totally constructive pleasure experienced during contemplative, superconscious meditation. Thus, inner peace which is not dependent upon externals is experienced. Sense urges are then more easily regulated and obsessive desire for activity without real purpose is neutralized. Our values change, we see life from a more reasonable perspective, and we are spontaneously inclined to modify our lifestyle to conform with worthy purposes and do all we can to contribute to our spiritual growth.

For persons who are able to meditate spontaneously, all that is usually required is for them to sit quietly and turn their attention to the contemplation of God, or to the highest, most comprehensible aspect of Reality. For others, preliminary procedures will be helpful.

It is always useful to pray when first sitting to meditate. As you do, open yourself to a relationship with God. God is the Oversoul, the cosmic Being. You are Godlike, you are a ray of pure consciousness, but you need a relationship with God because you are dwelling in the field of God in which everything is occurring. Sit upright, relaxed and comfortable, with closed eyes, and contemplate (and feel) the reality of God. Pray to experience your relationship with God. The relationship already exists, prayer can remove the mental and emotional barriers which prevent a clear perception of God. This may be all that is required in the way of procedure—to pray, then be still and wait in the silence—receptive, and open to inner response. This sitting, in a state of relaxed, alert awareness, is contemplation. Surrendered contemplation results in expanded awareness, soul satisfaction, subtle and fine perceptions, and intuitive insights. Sit for a long time in the silence, until you feel inclined to conclude the meditation session. You will know when to do this.

If further involvement of attention with a meditation technique is needed, or desired, use a mantra with which you feel comfortable. A mantra is a sound, or word-phrase, introduced in the mind to attract your attention and contribute to easy concentration. A convenient mantra, for persons of devotional temperament, is the word *God*. Just let your breathing flow naturally. Look gently into, and through, the space between your eyebrows. Look into the distance of inner space and contemplate the interior vastness. When inhalation occurs, let the word *God* float in your mind. When exhalation occurs, let the word *God* float in your mind. This is a gentle, easy, process which satisfies the soul. Continue to surrender to the process, looking within, listening within, giving yourself to meditation until your attention is internalized and the conscious use of the mantra ceases. Then rest in the deep silence for as long as you are inclined to do so.

Here are more specific guidelines to help you meditate with benefit. Choosing a time for meditation, and a quiet place where you will not be disturbed, proceed:

1. *Posture* – Sit upright and relaxed in a comfortable chair. If you are more comfortable sitting in a comfortable crosslegged posture, this is all right. But sit upright, to be alert and attentive to what you are doing and experienc-

ing. Look into the space between the eyebrows. Let your awareness be in the spinal pathway and higher brain. This will help you to more easily become internalized. Then withdraw your attention from body perceptions and focus it in the space between the eyebrows and in the higher brain.

2. *Begin* – While as relaxed as possible, breathe in and out a few times, just a little more deeply than usual, then let your breathing rhythm settle into a normal flow. Mentally pray, to attune your mind with God. Instead of praying "to God," feel that God is all around and, within, you. Feel that you are like a bubble in the cosmic sea. Pray "in God." Then be still and surrender to God's presence, looking gently within and "listening" to the inner silence. If you need an additional technique, to focus attention and avoid mental and emotional distractions, let the word *God* float in your mind as previously described. Dissolve in God. Let the boundaries of your ego fade away. When your mantra, or whatever technique you use, is no longer needed, let it drop away.

3. *Rest in the Silence* – Experience the calm and tranquility of conscious, thoughtless, meditation for as long as it persists or until you feel inclined to conclude your meditation session.

4. *Conclusion* – Sit for a short interlude to allow your meditative calm to be integrated with your thought processes, feelings, and body awareness. Then open your eyes and turn your attention to matters at hand.

It is recommended that at least 20 minutes be given to this practice, once or twice a day, for the purpose of stress reduction, deep relaxation, mental and emotional calm, and centering. Thus practiced, meditation can contribute to all of the benefits claimed for it. For deeper communion with the Infinite, and for more intentional contemplation for the purpose of improved understanding, you will want to sit for a longer duration.

After meditation, go about your usual living routine, inwardly calm and happy in your soul. After meditation, before getting up, you may want to engage in possibility-thinking, creative planning, visualization of desired outcomes, prayer for others and for world harmony, or for any other useful creative purpose.

If you are a beginning meditator, meditate as recommended on a regular schedule, without anxiety for immediate results, for at least six weeks to give yourself a chance to become proficient in practice and to determine useful results. Benefits are usually noticed within a few days but it is best not to overly analyze yourself or be preoccupied with whether or not your meditation practice is useful. Just include it in your daily routine and let the results unfold as they will.

While meditating, be surrendered to the process, and focused on your chosen ideal. If feelings and thoughts intrude, let them recede from your field of attention and remain intent upon your purpose. In time, feelings will become settled and thought processes will become refined so that you will no longer be distracted by them.

While gazing inward, you may perceive light in the space between your eyebrows, or a sense of luminous radiance in the skull cavity. If light is not perceived, do not feel that you are not progressing. Your increasing calmness, soul contentment and sense of attunement with God are more important. Initial light perception is due to the stimulation of the optic centers in the brain by the electrical activities manifesting there. You may also hear inner sounds: ringing in the ears, various alterations of the sound, or a sound which seems to have "substance" to it which is referred to by some as "the sound of inner silence." If you see inner light and hear inner sound, relax into it and let it fascinate your attention, while gently being inclined to determine its source. The ultimate source of all light and sound manifestation is the pure field of consciousness out of which all phenomena emerges. Contemplate that field of pure consciousness, the field of existence, and you will increasingly experience your nature as it.

Definitely avoid the temptation to be fascinated by

light and sound perceptions, by visions (the result of mental transformations) and by any other perceptions to the extent of being distracted from the purpose of meditation, which is to experience conscious awareness of being, or pure consciousness.

Now and then, meditate longer than usual, to provide yourself the opportunity to go more deeply into the creative silence. Occasionally, if convenient, meditate with friends who understand the process and who are proficient meditators. When meditating with friends, do not discuss personal experiences. Just meditate together to reinforce the inner experience.

Good times to meditate are early in the morning, before the mind becomes attracted to outer circumstances, and in the evening—either as a relaxing interlude between your work schedule and the evening's activities, or before going to sleep. When you go to sleep, think of God and melt in God.

Imagine All the Possibilities

One of the more remarkable gifts of the spirit we have, the exercise of which enables us to influence the course of events in our lives, is imagination. Examine carefully the following descriptions of the word *imagination*:

1. The act of forming mental images or concepts of what is not actually present at the time.
2. The faculty of forming such images or concepts.
3. The ability to reproduce images stored in the memory under the suggestions of associated images (*reproductive imagination*), or of recombining images of former experiences in the creation of new images different from any known by experience (*productive* or *creative imagination*).

I have emphasized several times in this text that our

Imagine All the Possibilities

states of consciousness and mental states determine the way we see the world, the way we see ourselves and how we relate to our environment. They determine our circumstances. This means that if we are desirous of having our circumstances changed, we have to make adjustments in perception and in mental states. Such adjustments may result in behavioral changes which are instrumental in influencing circumstances. It may also be, that even without behavioral changes, circumstances will change because of our capacity to see new possibilities and because life responds to our states of consciousness and mental states. Sometimes, obvious actions on our part are required, and at other times, they are not. With practice, you will learn when to act and when not to act, when to be outwardly involved and when to be still and let the forces of Nature respond to your imaginal acts.

Whenever you engage in possibility-thinking, you are using your imagination to envision desirable outcomes. The easiest way to proceed is to imagine possibilities, accept the ones which are most desirable, and assume that they will naturally unfold in divine order. When you do this (and you can), you will be able to predict your own future with accuracy. You may not always know the exact sequence of unfolding circumstances, but you will know final conclusions. You will walk with perfect faith. Should you occasionally compare how well life is unfolding for you, with how life used to be when you were not as conscious and trusting, you will be pleasantly amazed at the difference between the *you*, you are, and the *you* of former times. You may even want to share with others the way to more relaxed, more fulfilled living. Some will understand and be blessed. Many will not be able to comprehend, because their perception of themselves and their world is different. You will learn to see how it is possible for human beings to share a common environment, yet be separated by the distances between their respective levels of understanding.

At times, it may be difficult to be a possibility-thinker. Self-doubt, mental confusion, tiredness, the demands of challenging circumstances, negative attitudes and opinions of friends and acquaintances—can be disturbing influences. It is easier to be a possibility-thinker when self-confident, mentally alert, rested and energetic, when circumstances are supportive, and when we are self-determined instead of being subject to attitudes and behaviors of others. While entirely supportive inner and outer circumstances are ideal, they do not always prevail in our lives, and even in the face of challenge we can train ourselves to disregard distractions and elevate our consciousness to more optimum levels.

If your lifestyle is entirely supportive of your highest aspirations, you will more easily be a possibility-thinker. But regardless of circumstances, you can use *productive* or *creative* imagination to initiate changes in states of consciousness, mental states, physical states, and environmental circumstances. Just as with meditation practice, some of us are able to do it spontaneously and others find techniques helpful—so some of us are spontaneous possibility-thinkers and others find specific creative techniques helpful to get to the place where spontaneous possibility-thinking is natural. Therefore, for a more intentional and focused approach to using your faculty of creative imagination, practice as follows:

1. Whatever it is you need, want, want to do, experience, or see unfolded in your life, be very clear in your mind about it. Feel right about it and be certain that it is what you want as part of your life. It can be helpful to go over your notes to clarify your thinking and to be sure of your priorities. Then proceed with confidence.

2. Settle into a mood of quiet contemplation. Feel yourself to be merged in the presence of God and one with the universe. Feel yourself to be what you really are—a spiritual being, grounded in the Infinite. Rest in this awareness for a comfortable interlude.

3. In your mind's eye, picture yourself as being the person you desire to be, as having the circumstances you want to have. While thoughts of how circumstances may

unfold may come into your mind at this time, it is not necessary to actively speculate about the matter. The essential thing is to inwardly *see* and actually *feel* yourself as you want to be, as you want circumstances to be; that is, go to the end of the process, to the conclusion, and *see* and *feel* yourself there. *See* and *feel* "there" as "here," and "then" as "now."

4. Continue to so identify with the conclusion that you completely assume the *state of consciousness* and *feeling* that relates to your imaginal theme.

5. *Rest* in this realization. Be happy. Be thankful. Be fulfilled. When you are satisfied that you are completely settled in understanding, when you are soul content, let the practice session be concluded.

You may be inspired to do things to implement plans to help the creative process unfold. You may make changes in your life. You may be inclined not to do anything outwardly, either because you do not know what to do or because your guidance informs you that there is nothing you can, or need, to do. Just follow your guidance, while living out of the consciousness, the quiet acceptance, that what has been established within must unfold in an orderly way. And, it will. You are now functioning from a deeper level. You are grounded in the all pervasive field of consciousness out of which all things and circumstances unfold. You are in a cooperative relationship with the cosmic mental field which is the creative substance of all that is formed and without which nothing is formed. You are attuned to the Power that maintains the universe and It does the work.

Do not think in terms of using the Power, let It use you. Let It unfold circumstances in ways which are best for Its purposes and best for you and everyone who might be part of the completed unfoldment. Do your best to be sure that what you want, what you think you need, is in harmony with what is altogether good and constructive. In this way, you will be helping yourself to personal fulfillment while cooperating with life's purposes.

As you become more aware, more centered in God-realization, you will discover that you have but to be presented with a need to be met and life will meet it for you. The reason for this is that when you are established in soul peace, whenever that peace is even somewhat challenged because of personal need or because of the pressure of environmental circumstances, the universe will move to restore you to peace and make necessary adjustments to accomplish and maintain this condition. This is why persons who are inwardly settled in God-realization experience that their every need is met by the universe, as an act of grace.

You are supposed to be spiritually aware. You are supposed to be healthy-minded and knowledgeable. You are supposed to be emotionally well and mature. You are supposed to be physically healthy. You are supposed to enjoy wholesome, supportive relationships. You are supposed to fulfill worthy purposes. You are supposed to be prosperous: to thrive, to flourish and be successful—not in just some ways, but in all ways. You are supposed to experience inner peace, spiritual growth and the fulfillment of life's purposes. Therefore, possibility-thinking and right use of creative imagination should be understood as productive processes you can use to participate in life's plan for you.

You can, when engaged in possibility-thinking and the exercise of creative imagination, be general or specific in focus. The general way is to imagine, assume and accept total fulfillment which includes every aspect of your life. However, if life is flowing well and there are but a few obvious challenges, focus on these areas and clear them. Problems common to the human condition are: personal insecurity in spite of outer pretense to the contrary, loneliness, lack of money and other necessary resources, uncertainty about what to do with our lives, dependency upon substances or relationships, poor work habits or undisciplined behavior, unresolved trauma related to past experiences, inability to accomplish worthy purposes, unbearably restricting environmental circumstances, and physical illness, to name but a few. All are grounded in lack of understanding.

Our problems are often due to self-centeredness, laziness, insufficient knowledge about how to improve our circumstances, general behaviors which are not supportive of purposeful outcomes, stress, poor nutrition, unconscious tendencies with which we have not come to terms or resolved, lack of discernment, and falsely assuming that what is normal for the majority of people in human consciousness is also true of us. What is needed, in such circumstances, is self-education and constructive changes in attitude and behavior.

If you have problem areas in your life which interfere with function, use possibility-thinking and creative imagination to *see* and *feel* yourself as you want to be, as you can be. *Be* like that, *think* like that, *act* like that, *live* like that. Your thinking, knowing, feeling, behavior, and experiences flow from your awareness of *being*. *Having* and *expressing* are in direct relationship to your awareness of *being*. Imagine yourself as problem-free. How would it be to be problem-free? Imagine all useful possibilities! Train yourself not to whine, complain, justify purposeless behavior, rationalize limitations, or to indulge in moods and other destructive behaviors. Come to terms with the fact that you have to grow up sometime, you have to be emotionally mature eventually—why not now?

If You Need Healing, Do These Things

If you need healing, the only thing that really needs to be healed, is your understanding.

The major causes of dysfunction, disease and death among the general population are self-inflicted. (I am not including the genetically impaired or the obviously psychotic, though not all of these are beyond help.) Accidents, a leading cause of suffering and death, are largely avoidable. Major diseases, including heart disease and other complications of the cardiovascular system, diabetes, and cancer are largely avoidable and often curable. Infectious diseases are, likewise, for the most part avoidable and curable. It is estimated that at least 70 percent of the common ailments for which people seek help would be resolved without treatment of any kind, because of the body's innate inclination to restore itself to balance. The majority of physical ailments are preventable by choosing a healthy lifestyle, managing stress, avoiding worry and other psychological conflicts, and by the implementation of a sensible food plan.

A major need in today's world is for people to be educated in matters pertaining to healthy living and to be more responsible for their own wellness. When help is needed, one should of course have recourse to the most reliable assistance possible. If you need help in helping yourself to wellness, get help. Do not indulge in illusory thinking and continue in that confused state to pretend that you are too good, too "spiritual," to ask for help when it is obviously needed.

Where there is disharmony, there is the possibility of disease. Symptoms not always obvious to casual observation may exist at deeper levels and cause problems in the future. When psychological conflicts become pronounced, disappointment or trauma is experienced; when stress accumulates, when the immune system becomes weakened, when the future looks hopeless, when the accumulated effects of wrong diet of other self-destructive behaviors mount, the deeper causes of disharmony can manifest as disease symptoms. Wellness must then be restored and to avoid future problems, harmony must be maintained.

It is well known that the intentional cultivation of constructive attitudes, such as faith, hope, love, and optimism actually contribute to internal harmony and to the production and secretion of internal substances which support wellness. Also, fear, despair, hate, envy, moodiness, guilt, purposelessness, loneliness, and the like contribute to internal disharmony and weaken the body's immune system. Faith, positive belief, can trigger the healing responses of the body, just as it can beneficially influence changes in relationships and circumstances.

Since life is an organic whole, we are not separate from any part of the universe. As spiritual beings, we are expressions of the only life there is, God. Through the medium of our minds we participate, consciously or unconsciously, with universal or cosmic mind, God's mind. Our bodies are formed of the ingredients of Nature but we are not confined to our bodies, or our minds, except as we are conditioned to be; our consciousness pervades the universe and its energies flow through us.

Harmony can be restored, and maintained, by a variety of practical means so that mental, emotional and physical wellness is normal. The importance of spiritual awareness should not be neglected if total wellness is to be experienced, and a wise physician will include every aspect of a patient's life in his diagnoses and treatment of disease. An ancient Ayurvedic* text affirms: "When treating the patient there is nothing in the field of Nature which cannot be considered as medicine." A truly holistic approach is best, including: the importance of spiritual awareness, mental and emotional factors, rest, diet, meditation, cleansing and detoxification procedures, and whatever else may be necessary to facilitate the healing process. It is understood that the treatment alone does not cure, appropriate treatment and patient-care provide supportive circumstances in which the all-radiant healing forces of Nature can be freely expressive. Life heals: we only do those things which are helpful in allowing it to fulfill its innate inclinations.

When our thought processes are well ordered, when

---

* Ayurveda (life-knowledge) is a system of wellness with an estimated three to five thousand year history, developed in India and still the wellness regimen of choice by the majority of its population. In recent years Ayurveda has become more well known in the United States and Europe where it is being researched and applied.

our emotional states are harmonized, when our physical needs are met, and when the will to live is present and influential, we will be inclined to help ourselves in practical ways. More, when we are open to help, the universe obviously assists us by bringing to our attention opportunities which are life-supporting and information which is useful to our needs.

If you are presently radiantly healthy (and I hope you are), maintain your wellness by remaining in tune with life and living with purpose. If you need healing, do the necessary things to assist the healing process and put the challenge behind you.

Often we are not obviously aware of contributing causes of disease or discomfort, especially those causes rooted in emotional discontent because of inharmonious relationships with our environment or with other people. Other people are not the cause of our problems; our problems are not their fault. True, we can be influenced by other people, but when we are self-responsible we can remove ourselves from their influences and we can heal any condition which may be the result of past unpleasant relationships. To continue to blame others "for what they did to us" is to dramatize the role of being a victim of circumstances, instead of doing the necessary work on ourselves to become functional. If we choose to do so, we can remain dysfunctional for years by refusing to change our states of consciousness, mental and emotional states, and behavior, but that wouldn't be a wise choice. If there are conflicts because of inharmonious relationships we can: 1) heal the relationship, if possible; 2) terminate the relationship, if necessary; 3) heal ourselves of any destructive results of such relationships. Anger, resentment, guilt, feelings of being unloved, fear of having relationships because of past unpleasant experiences—can not only contribute to internal disharmony and possible illness, but will almost certainly interfere with behavior and prevent us from experiencing the human happiness and fulfillment we deserve. We do violence to ourselves when we allow mental unrest and psychological pain to persist. The most direct route out of undesirable circumstances is to choose attitudes, feelings, and behaviors which contribute to desirable circumstances. Instead of focusing on what was, or what is, the constructive approach is to actualize what can be.

For self-care, maintain a supportive lifestyle and do all of the practical things you know to do to help yourself live as you should live. Do the things you learn about and feel would be helpful to you. For professional help, seek out the best qualified, spiritually oriented person you can find to help you. For any assistance which may be required to improve your understanding, seek out the most competent, the best qualified, the most actualized and spiritually aware person you can find to assist you.

In this book, you have many of the helpful procedures you can use to help yourself. Whatever else you may need, your inner guidance and God's grace will provide. The universe will always meet you at your level of legitimate need and sincere desire when you are open to it.

The main thing is to proceed from spiritual understanding and soul conviction and to settle for nothing less than what is possible for you to experience. If you see yourself as weak, inept, and incapable of worthwhile change, your experiences will tend to reflect your opinion of yourself. If you see yourself as you really are—a spiritual being for whom all things are possible—your perception and experiences will reinforce your realizations and expectations.

If you are spiritually unaware and have mistaken ideas about God and your purpose in life, you are in need of healing.

If you are not seeing your world correctly and are maintaining erroneous concepts and opinions, you are in need of healing.

If you are emotionally disturbed, you are in need of healing.

If you are dramatizing neurotic behavior, you are in need of healing.

If you are not on good terms with people, you are in need of healing.

If you are not physically well, you are in need of healing.

If you are dependent upon substances, behavior, or destructive relationships, you are in need of healing.

If you are self-righteous, narrow-minded, or prejudiced, you are in need of healing.

If you lack clear purpose and feel that life is devoid of meaning, you are in need of healing.

If you are not prospering in all ways, you are in need of healing.

If you are not happy, thankful for the gift of life and in the flow of grace, you are in need of healing.

Come to terms with how life is for you now, and if you are in need of healing, see to it. And with any process you use, be sure to include an ample measure of commonsense.

Your Body is the Temple in Which God Dwells

Your body is a sacred temple in which the spirit of God dwells. How clean, ordered, and functional is your body temple? How responsive is your body to your needs? How responsive is your body to the inclination of soul consciousness to express more fully through it? How attuned are you to the rhythms of the universe?

Healthy, long life not only allows our sojourn in this world to be enjoyable, it provides the basis for us to fulfill all of our worthy purposes. Our needs can be more easily met when we are healthy. Relationships can be more satisfying. More useful service can be rendered. God-realization can be more easily experienced, sustained, and expressed when our health is good and the nervous system is unstressed and refined.

Not only does our consciousness express through the body, but our consciousness and soul forces interact with cosmic forces which flow through the field of Nature and nurture evolutionary processes. Therefore, the healthier we are, the easier it is to experience spiritual growth and be responsive to evolutional forces which can assist us toward growth and fulfillment.

Just as God, the cosmic soul, is superior to cosmic mind and the manifest universe, we, as spiritual beings, are superior to the mind and body we use. When we are spiritually aware and knowledgeable about how the mind operates and the body functions, we can more easily direct the operations of the mind and utilize the body for higher purposes. Unfortunately, some who are otherwise sincere on the spiritual path neglect the body, or even abuse it. They may mistakenly assume the body to be a burdensome inconvenience. A person of understanding will accept the fact of physical incarnation as an opportunity to experience life and to grow in wisdom.

At birth, the body is endowed with constitutional characteristics provided by the parents, and influenced by environmental conditions, personal soul awareness and psychological states. Physical birth is not the beginning of our relationship with the universe, it is merely another incident in a chain of such events. Our basic physical constitution remains with us throughout our span of Earth-life, although it can be modified in a variety of ways. Prenatal influences can somewhat determine our condition at birth; the behavior and environment of our parents (especially the mother), foods and other substances ingested by the mother, and the psychological states of our parents. Circumstances following birth can be determining factors such as: whether or not the child is nurtured and provided emotional support, proper nourishment and other care essential to its needs. There is nothing we can do about how we were provided for when we were very young, but there is much we can do now that we are able to choose for ourselves.

The constructive spiritual and psychological tendencies we brought with us into this world can be further cultivated. Self-limiting tendencies can be weakened and eliminated. Of extreme importance, for one who is resolved to unfold and actualize inner capacities, is to make right choices and focus only upon matters essential to higher ends. Self-defeating attitudes and behaviors should definitely be renounced. A common self-defeating attitude frequently expressed is, "I'm what I am and conditions are what they are, so I might as well accept the facts and get by as best I can." Instead, affirm with soul conviction and positive resolve, "I am made in the image and likeness of God, a spiritual being in a spiritual universe. All things possible are available to me!"

The "biological fire" responsible for life processes, for our appearance, our strength, our energy, our growth and maturity, for our life essence and radiance can be nurtured and increased in influence. This occurs naturally as we live in harmony with the rhythms of Nature and open ourselves to higher influences.

Provide for yourself a lifestyle which is entirely supportive. Reduce psychological and physiological stress by living an ordered life. Meditate on a regular schedule. If your life is disorganized, if stress is allowed to accumulate, if spiritual growth is neglected, everything else you do to assist yourself to wellness will be only partially effective. Zest for life, good nutrition, exercise, enjoyable relationships, personal accomplishment, good deeds—these are all useful—but more is needed. The "more" that is needed, is to nourish the inner being and open consciousness to the Higher Power, to God.

Provide for yourself a living (and work) environment which is clean, quiet and devoid of stress-causing influences. Your home environment should be pleasant, comfortable and free from environmental pollution. While it may not always be possible to completely determine your work and social environments, at least train yourself to remain inwardly calm and undisturbed by your surroundings, including the behaviors and conversations of others. As you grow spiritually and experience the unfoldment of life's purposes for you, you will discover that your environment, including the people with whom you work and associate on a social basis, will become increasingly ordered and supportive. You will choose to create environments which are supportive and you will attract circumstances which conform with your choices.

Nourish your body with pure, natural foods. A vegetarian food plan is best, because the human body is designed to process grains, legumes, vegetables, fruits and seeds (nuts and other plant seeds). This is obvious by an examination of human tooth structure, length of the intestinal tract, and the fact that when we are healthy we naturally prefer such a diet.

Your exercise program can be a matter of personal choice, but do have one. Brisk walking for a mile or more a day, tennis, cycling, swimming—and any reasonable program that will stimulate breathing and cardiovascular function is recommended, at least three times a week. Also useful are more relaxed routines such as Tai Chi, Hatha Yoga and similar procedures. The more energetic exercise routines strengthen the body and increase energy reserves. The quieter routines improve muscle tone, stimulate glands, improve blood, lymph and cerebro-spinal fluid circulation, refine the nervous system and keep open the centers in the body through which vital and cosmic forces circulate. Through the latter centers, cosmic forces which are not-yet-material flow into the body and become more pronounced in character and influence. If you are intent upon spiritual growth, a daily routine of Hatha Yoga, a few simple pranayamas (life-force balancing procedures), followed by superconscious meditation, is highly recommended.

I am also an advocate of chiropractic adjustments for restoring and maintaining internal body balance. I have a chiropractic adjustment once a month for this purpose. You don't have to have a "back problem" to enjoy the benefits of chiropractic adjustments.

How long we live through the physical body is determined by our basic constitution, our degree of wellness, our purpose for being here, and our expectations. Since soul awareness is superior to mental operations and body function, our intentions should be the determining factors for how, and how long, we live in this world in health and with purpose. Right living, right purpose, and spiritual awareness, can result in a healthy, long, and fulfilling life. The biological aging processes are slowed when life is lived well. One should then move from infancy to youth, to adulthood and extended middle-age, and depart the body during advanced years without experiencing any of the complications so common to many. By reducing psychological conflicts, managing stress, maintaining a constructive mental attitude, and doing everything else required, one should easily remain healthy and active for as long as one has purpose for being in this world. One-hundred and twenty years is now considered the possible normal life span for a human being. Knowing this, it is unfortunate that so many people retire from active, purposeful involvement when they are only 60 or 65 years of age, and that many fear old age and death.

It is natural to experience progressive transition-stages which occur along with growth and maturity, but spiritual growth should continue through every stage of Earth-life and accelerate during the later years. So take good care of your body temple and it will serve you well. When you have fulfilled your purposes, including that of attaining the highest realization of God possible, the body can be discarded and returned to the elements of Nature and the field of cosmic forces from which it was formed. You, in subtle, fine and transcendent spheres, will live forever.

The One Hour a Day that Can Anchor Your Life in the Infinite

A ship anchored at sea will not easily be removed from its place by the shifting tides and sometimes storms which may prevail about it. Likewise, when your life is anchored in the Infinite, you will not be unduly disturbed by the currents and challenges which may be encountered.

Can just one hour a day really make a difference? Yes, it can. As we relate to the world, it can happen that we become too involved with, and dependent upon, externals. As a result, we are moved away from our center, the awareness of being, poised, alert, and flawlessly perceptive. We may then be inclined to find something outside ourselves to hold onto—a relationship, a project, a belief system, or behaviors which are not always entirely constructive. We are then coping, but we are not being successful in experiencing the fulfillment of life's purposes.

What is needed, then, is something we can do by ourselves, something we choose to do which is entirely constructive. This provides us the opportunity to be in control of our lives, without any external thing or circumstance being influential. Many functional people already do this. They schedule regular regimens which are not related to their usual routines—such as an exercise program at a health club, wholesome social activities, an outing with family or friends, a visit to a museum or to the theater, time given to a hobby, a relaxing interlude in the yard or garden, or time alone with a good book. These can be refreshing interludes of rest, renewal, and learning. But there is something else we can do, which is very personal, very private, and which will definitely contribute to peace of soul and spiritual growth. I am referring to the one hour a day (at least) we devote to our personal wellness and spiritual growth. A recommended routine follows. You can modify it to suit your personal needs. Do this the first thing upon awakening in the morning, or at any convenient one-hour interlude you choose.

1. Go to the bathroom, eliminate body wastes and refresh yourself. If a morning routine, rinse your mouth and brush your teeth. Shower if you want to, or do this after your routine.

2. Do your Hatha Yoga routine (or your preferred gentle exercise routine). Conclude with a few minutes of alternate nostril breathing. (To do this: sit upright and relaxed. Exhale. With your finger, close your right nostril and inhale through the left nostril, rather deeply but don't overdo it. Close the left nostril and exhale slowly and easily through the right nostril. Inhale through the right nostril and exhale through the left one. Pause momentarily after inhalation and exhalation. Repeat this pranayama routine five to ten times.) This practice will help to balance the flows of prana (vital force) in the body, clear the mind, and help you relax.

3. Pray and meditate.

After meditation, you may want to read inspirational material while your mind is clear and you are receptive to learning. Or you can do this later, at a more convenient time.

An optional addition to your schedule, daily or a few times a week, is to massage your body with sesame or olive oil before your shower. To do this, warm the oil in a metal or ceramic cup (about a quarter of a cup will do). Massage the oil into your hair and scalp, then your face, neck, shoulders, upper back, arms and hands, chest, abdomen, lower back, groin, thighs, lower legs, and feet. Massage carefully and deeply into each foot, to work out any tightness or soreness. (It's a good idea to have a bath mat or rough towel in the bathtub to avoid slipping on any oil that may be there.) This regimen, besides being an enjoyable self-care experience, helps to balance the body's subtle forces which, in turn, regulate the constituent elements of its constitution.

In addition to your daily routine, it is recommended that you schedule one evening a week, and sometimes an entire weekend, for inspirational reading, gentle exercise, and longer meditation. Consider this special routine a personal spiritual retreat experience.

Once a year, at least, go to a private place near a seashore, or in the mountains or a rural area, for a several day spiritual retreat. You may select a facility where support activities are provided, such as classes, workshops, meditation sessions and other useful programs. While doing this, allow plenty of time for private inner work and rest. This should not be an occasion for restless social interaction, for this would be contrary to the purpose of being on a spiritual retreat. If it is not always possible to go somewhere for this purpose, then stay home and create a supportive environment where you are.

If your domestic or work schedule prevents you from having an hour in the morning for your routine, at least meditate before starting the day's activities, and attend to a more complete routine later in the day when it is more convenient for you. But it is a good idea to train yourself to go to bed early, and to awaken early for your quiet time. The rest of your day will flow more smoothly, you will be more calm and centered, and more conscious and purposeful.

*Be Good to the Universe and the
Universe Will be Good to You*

Life is inclined to orderly completion of its purposes. You have only to learn to cooperate with it.

The universe is self-regulating, self-supporting and self-renewing. You have only to be open to it.

As a specialized expression of pure consciousness, you are already perfect, knowledgeable and free. You have only to consciously know this and express it.

The Power that manifests the universe is entirely benevolent. Everything needed for the self-fulfilling processes of life to complete their purposes is within the field of Nature at gross, subtle and fine levels. Therefore, you have only to learn to relate to the Power that nourishes the universe, to experience inner peace, spiritual growth and the fulfillment of life's purposes.

There is a place within you, where you are one with the Infinite. This is the place from which all knowledge, all creativity, all supply flows into expression in your personal experience. Although change and transformation continually occurs in the universe and in your personal affairs, ultimate conclusions are always in harmony with what is highest and best. This is why we pronounce the universe as benevolent, as good—and why grace always prevails.

When you are good to yourself, good to others and good to the universe, it is easier for the universe to be good to you. The ideal way to live is to renounce behaviors which are self-limiting and to cultivate behaviors which are consciousness-expanding. This is the path of enlightened living.

To be enlightened is to be consciously knowledgeable. Spontaneous living and its results, naturally follow.

Write Your Possible Futures, with Love

One of the most compelling, creative things you can do is to consciously and intentionally write your hopes, dreams, aspirations and specific plans to contribute to their actualization. Writing in this way clarifies your thinking,

focuses your attention, commits you to the creative process and more fully attunes your mind and being to the Infinite. Idle daydreaming, half-hearted wishing, mood-influenced behavior and procrastination are counterproductive and deny us the results we deserve. Overcome intellectual laziness, one of the chief causes of failure, by giving regular attention to writing your possible futures, with love. Yes, with love. Because you are a good person, life is good, and whatever you do should be thought of as manifesting goodness.

To conclude this section I have provided forms for you to use, to enable you to participate in your own unfoldment and spiritual growth. I recommend that you copy them in a notebook so that your creative involvements can be more easily and generously expressed. I find it convenient to have available several large-format lined-paper notepads. This allows ample provision for journal entries, possibility-thinking notations and for writing ideas as they come to mind. Keep your writing materials in a private place, for your use only. An exception to this would be if you are doing some of your creative planning in partnership with others with whom you have entered into a working relationship for the purpose of mutual support in joint-ventures. But for your inner work, you will still want to keep your writings private, between you and God alone.

Write during quiet interludes, when you are calm and centered, removed from possible outside distractions. This may be during the early morning hours, after meditative contemplation, or at any other time when you are removed from circumstances which might interfere with concentration. (I write on my notepads when I first get to my office in the morning, in the late afternoon before concluding the office workday, on airplanes when traveling to and from lecture engagements, in hotel rooms, and at home during evening relaxation time.)

Copy the forms in your notebook as they are outlined in these pages. Fill them out completely, including your own personalized written affirmation where indicated. In all ways, be intentional. Allow plenty of extra pages for jotting down ideas and for listing options and possibilities. Because your perception of your world and yourself will change, and because life processes are continuously unfolding, you will want to review the completed forms from time to time and make changes as your understanding increases and as guidance determines.

To help yourself visualize desired outcomes and completed projects, cut out pictures and photographs from magazines and other sources and include them in your notebook along with your written plans. The idea is not only to maintain clear mental concepts but to also add the vital ingredient of feeling, so that what you want to express in your life is firmly established in your consciousness.

Do every practical thing you know to do, to help yourself accomplish your worthy purposes. Do not be reluctant to do these things. At times, you may wonder whether or not you are merely fooling yourself, that perhaps you are indulging in fantasy and pretense. The truth of the matter is, if you are not actualizing your divine abilities you are pretending to be unable to do so, for one reason or another. So if you are going to pretend, why not pretend that you are wise, capable and accomplished? Why not use your creative abilities to know your real nature and to express without limitations as you are meant to do?

When writing, feel yourself to be what you are—a spiritual being in a spiritual universe, grounded in the Infinite and open to all things possible. Know that you are in partnership with the Infinite and that It nourishes you and expresses through and around you to the degree that you are open and responsive. Know that so long as you are surrendered to life's purposes and your aspirations are righteous (in harmony with natural law), nothing is impossible to you—because nothing is impossible to God.

NOTE: As you proceed, it can be helpful to refer to sections in the preceding text which relate to the theme being focused upon during your creative writing project.

#1
Write Your Life Mission Statement

If our life is to have direction we must know why we are here and what our purpose (mission) is. After prayerful contemplation and quiet thought, *clearly* write your major worthy purposes to be fulfilled in this lifetime. Be as specific as you can. (Use this form, also, when planning any major venture, such as starting a business, organizing a project or becoming involved in any useful situation. Know why you are doing what you do and let your priorities be chosen accordingly.)

My mission is _____

_____

_____

_____

_____

_____

_____

_____

_____

Affirm Aloud With
Feeling and Conviction

"Understanding that I am a spiritual being in a spiritual universe, I trust in God while using my inborn creative abilities to be open to life and experience the fulfillment of my life's purposes. I do my best to help myself, while being responsive to higher guidance and evidence of abundant grace."

Every believer in this world of ours must be a spark of light, a center of love, a vivifying leaven amidst his fellowmen, and he will be all this more perfectly the more closely he lives in communion with God and in the intimacy of his own soul.
POPE JOHN XXIII (1881-1963)
Pacem in Terris

Well, I dreamed
That stone by stone I rear'd a sacred
 fane,
A temple, neither Pogoda, Mosque, nor
 Church,
But loftier, simpler, always open-door'd
To every breath from heaven, and Truth
 and Peace
And Love and Justice came and dwelt
 therein.
ALFRED LORD TENNYSON (1809-1892)
Akbar's Dream

At fifteen my mind was bent on learning; at thirty, I stood firm; at forty, I was free from delusions; at fifty, I understood the will of God; at sixty, my ears were receptive to the truth; at seventy, I could follow the promptings of my heart without overstepping the boundaries of right.
CONFUCIUS (551-479 B.C.)
Analects

The Masters say that the soul has two faces. The higher one always sees God, the lower one looks downward and informs the senses. The higher one is the summit of the soul, it gazes into eternity.
MEISTER ECKHART (1260-1327)
Sermons

#2
Write Your Hopes and Dreams, with Love
(for yourself, others and your world)

Be a possibility-thinker. Let your imagination and your divine aspiration be unbounded. Whatever you can imagine and believe, if possible to be manifested in the realm of Nature, can unfold on the screen of time and space. See only the highest and best, only entirely constructive outcomes.

For myself: _____

_____

_____

_____

For others: _____

_____

_____

_____

For Planet Earth: _____

_____

_____

"Joyfully, I envision all wonderful circumstances possible for myself, for others and for Planet Earth. I see the good and bless it. I see the good and invite it into obvious manifestation. I allow divine attributes to be actualized in my life and acknowledge them in all people and all ideal circumstances."

#3
A Specific Program for Spiritual Growth

What do you need to do to contribute to your spiritual growth? _____

_____

_____

What have you been doing that interferes with spiritual growth and which you will (from now on) eliminate from your life? (Included may be self-centered behavior, procrastination, indulging in fantasy, dependent behavior of any kind, negative thinking, allowing moods to determine behavior, clinging to illusions, and so on.) _____

_____

_____

_____

What will you do *specifically* to order your life and help yourself to psychological and spiritual growth? _____

_____

_____

_____

What worthwhile religious, philosophical, or metaphysical study program do you now have (or will implement immediately)? _____

_____

_____

Write, with Love

Write your daily routine for prayer, meditation and contemplation: _____

_____
_____
_____
_____
_____
_____
_____

Write your own personalized affirmation to support your practices: _____

_____
_____
_____
_____
_____
_____
_____
_____

The soul, when it shall have driven away from itself all that is contrary to the Divine Will, becomes transformed in God in love —the soul then becomes immediately enlightened by and transformed in God, because He communicated His own supernatural being in such a way that the soul seems to be God Himself and to possess the things of God, the soul seems to be God rather than itself and indeed is God by participation.
SAINT JOHN OF THE CROSS (1542-1591)
The Ascent of Mount Carmel

Use me, God in Thy great harvest field,
Which stretcheth far and wide like a wide
    sea:
The gatherers are so few; I fear the
    precious yield
Will suffer loss. Oh, find a place for me!
CHRISTINA ROSSETTI (1830-1894)
Send Me

Once my understanding was let down into the bottom of the sea, and there I saw green hills and valleys, with the appearance of moss strewn with seaweed and gravel. Then I understood in this way: that if a man or woman were there under the wide waters, if they could see God, as God is continually with man, they would be safe in soul and body, and come to no harm.
JULIAN OF NORWICH (1343-1416)
Showings

A pagan lady asked Rabbi Jose, "Can your God draw near to Him whom He wills?" He brought her a basket of figs. She chose a good one and ate it. He said to her, "You know how to choose. Should not God know how to choose? Him who He sees to be a doer of good deeds He chooses and brings near to Him."
The Talmud

#4
Your "one hour a day" Self-Care Routine

This can include everything you routinely do on a daily schedule to contribute to wellness, peace of mind and inner growth. Included can be personal hygiene regimens, grooming, exercise, meditation, study, and whatever else you find useful. ___

#5
Physical Wellness and Vitality Program

Write your program to self-responsibly contribute to your physical wellness, vitality and function. Heal conditions that can be healed, maintain ideal body weight, obtain adequate rest, exercise regularly, choose a sensible food plan, schedule regular visits to your dentist and any other health professional whose knowledge and services may be helpful to you.

Where improvement is needed: _____

_____

_____

_____

Procedures implemented to experience improvement:

_____

_____

_____

Usual bedtime: _____ Usual awakening time: _____

Daily ( ) or several times a week (when?) exercise program. This can include walking, Hatha Yoga, any other suitable exercise.

Exercise routine: _____

_____

_____

Conscious choice food plan (a natural, vegetarian diet is best):_____

_____

_____

_____

_____

_____

Supplemental procedures (chiropractic adjustments, bodywork, ayurveda therapy, etc.):_____

_____

_____

_____

NOTE: Remain aware of the spirit-mind-body relationship. Spiritual awareness and conscious cultivation of faith, hope, optimism, thankfulness and cheerfulness awaken and liberate healing forces in the body and strengthens the body's immune system. The purpose of healthy, long life is to allow you to fulfill your worthy purposes and to allow life's purposes to be fulfilled through you.

Read helpful books and literature and obtain necessary information about diet, exercise, mental attitude and all matters relating to wellness. See the resource section in the back of this book.

If you have real purpose in life, it will be much easier to attend to all matters which can contribute to function.

#6
Enjoyable Life-Enhancing Activities

These may include anything you feel inclined to do which will afford learning opportunities, the cultivation of talents, improving your skills and in making life more enjoyable and meaningful for you. Also included, may be community service, participation in worthwhile activities and projects, vacations, travel, language learning, art, music, special research projects, and so on. _____

#7
Worthy Projects to be Actualized

Include long-term and short-term projects. Long-term projects will enable you to plan accordingly and short-term projects, when completed, will provide satisfaction and improve self-confidence. Projects should be worthwhile, clearly defined and progressively actualized. For each project (or goal), write what you feel you will need to do to contribute to its unfoldment. Also write what you feel may be present obstacles (if any) to the actualization of your projects and what you can do to eliminate the obstacles (whether they be in your own mind or actual existing circumstances). Your list can include the primary aims of life as well as whatever else you honestly feel is useful to the fulfillment of your worthy purposes.

List the project first; then what you feel you need to do to contribute to its completion. This will probably require several pages of notes and occasional reworking, as former projects are actualized and new ones are formulated and agreed upon. If you are writing on this page you may want to merely list the projects, then transfer them to your notebook for more detailed planning. _____

_____

_____

_____

_____

NOTE: After deciding upon your project, arm yourself with all of the useful information you can obtain relative to how to proceed. Seek the advice of competent persons when you can, either in person or through books and other sources. Learn what to do and *what not to do* to be successful in fulfilling your plans.

#8
Cultivating a Prosperity Consciousness

To *prosper* is "to thrive, to flourish and to be successful" in all worthy ventures and activities. To do this you will have to be on friendly terms with the universe, to allow yourself to be nourished by it and to wisely use its available resources. To live life as it is meant to be lived, we should be prosperous spiritually, mentally, emotionally, in relationships, in worthy endeavors and in accord with life's purposes for us.

If you do not have a prosperity consciousness, an open and understanding attitude about being able to thrive, to flourish, and to be successful in worthy ventures and all of life's expressions, what are the attitudes and feelings that you have which cause conflict?_____

_____

_____

_____

What can (and will) you do to eliminate these attitudes and feelings (including the behaviors which they manifest)?_____

_____

_____

_____

Do you have a prudent savings plan ( ) yes ( ) no
If not, implement one immediately, putting an agreed upon percentage of your income into a *secure* money growth plan. What percentage of your income will you save in this manner on a regular schedule?_____

Do you have a tithing or giving schedule? ( ) yes ( ) no
If not, just as *regularly* as you invest your personal savings, also give to worthy causes, freely and with gratitude. This does not have to actually be one-tenth (a tithe), it should be whatever you honestly feel good about and which is appropriate. This can be given to religious, philosophical, cultural and humanitarian causes in which you believe and which contribute to the spiritual education, welfare and uplift of society and individuals. What percentage will you give in these ways? _____
To what causes? _____

_____

Live simply. Avoid debt. Spend wisely, without waste. Treat all resources with respect and relate to others and your world with reverence. The field of Nature (the world in which we live) is sacred. It provides us with everything we need to flourish and fulfill our purposes. Be sure that all of your activities, including those which are directly related to financial matters, have constructive outcomes for yourself, others who are involved, and for the planet.

What other things can you do to cultivate a prosperity consciousness? _____

_____

_____

Write an affirmation that expresses your prosperity consciousness: _____

_____

_____

_____

#9
A Comprehensive Life-Plan

Regardless of your age or the circumstances of the moment, if you will clearly write your life-plan you will immediately enter into a more conscious relationship with the creative forces of the universe. You will become more expansive and will see yourself in relationship to the world in a more cosmic way. Feel free to amend your plans as your understanding increases and new insights dawn.

From where you are now, what do you see yourself doing for the remainder of this incarnation? _____

_____

_____

_____

If you are on purpose, continue. If not, what do you need to do to define your priorities and focus your life? (Do these things). _____

_____

_____

_____

What do you need to do to acquire necessary knowledge and improve your skills? (Do these things.) _____

_____

_____

_____

Write, with Love

If you are a young adult, open your mind to all possibilities and prepare yourself accordingly. You can have a wonderful future as your capacities unfold and as God leads.

If you are at the mid-point in your life, you still have much to do and experience, and necessary changes can be made in divine order.

If you are in your twilight years, spend more time in prayer, meditation and divine contemplation.

If you have property or possessions, make a valid will and let responsible persons know where it is. Complete all projects and fulfill all obligations before departing this world.

Whatever you feel is worthy of you, whatever you feel is of value, know it can unfold harmoniously. You may begin by planning from a limited (conditioned) point of view, but as your continue to contemplate your life-plan a sense of destiny will pervade your mind and consciousness and you will be intuitively led to make right choices. You will become increasingly open to higher guidance and grace.

Remember, always, to plan in terms of life's purposes and not in small, self-centered ways. You are a ray of divine life, a spiritual being involved in a changing drama. The real you is omniscient and immortal. Let the real you express. As you progress, you will notice that life is working things out for you, rather than you having to contrive to always be in charge. Be responsible, then let go and let God.

What else can you do to contribute to the unfoldment of your worthy life-plan? _____

_____

_____

#10
An Affirmation of All Things Possible

After an interlude of quiet contemplation, write an affirmation in simple, concise words that best expresses your present understanding of your relationship with God and the universe, and your role in life. Let it confirm your conviction, your realization and your conscious choice to live from now on with an All Things Possible attitude, and with a lifestyle which is fully supportive of your worthy dreams and highest aspirations: _____

_____

_____

_____

_____

_____

_____

_____

_____

_____

_____

_____

_____

Epilogue

Answers to Often Asked Questions

Our union with a Being whose activity is world-wide and who dwells in the heart of humanity cannot be a passive one. In order to be united with Him we have to divest our work of selfishness and become *Visvakarma*, "the world-worker," we must work for all. In order to be one with this Mahatma, "the Great Soul," one must cultivate the greatness of soul which identifies itself with the soul of all peoples and not merely with that of one's own.

RABINDRANATH TAGORE (1861-1941)
The Religion of Man

The king was seated in a garden, and one of his counselors was speaking of the wonderful works of God. "Show me a sign," said the king, "and I will believe." "Here are four acorns," said the counselor: "will your majesty plant them in the ground, and then stoop down for a moment and look into this clear pool of water." The king did so. "Now," said the other, "look up." The king looked up and saw four oak-trees where he had planted the acorns. "Wonderful!" he exclaimed; "this is indeed a work of God." "How long were you looking into the water?" asked the counselor. "Only a second," said the king. "Eighty years have passed as a second," said the other. The king looked at his garments; they were threadbare. He looked at his reflection in the water; he had become an old man. "There is no miracle here, then," he said angrily. "Yes," said the other; "it is God's work, whether he do it in one second or eighty years."

BORDEN P. BOWNE (1847-1910)
The Immanence of God

We can usually determine satisfying solutions to our problems by clearly defining them and then using our intelligence and common sense. If insight is not immediately forthcoming, we can open ourselves more fully to life and expect it to meet our needs, and it will. We may experience episodes of intuitive discovery, circumstances may unfold in a more supportive way, or we may be led to helpful sources of information. The following questions are among those I am frequently asked. My answers may not be the final word in every instance, but they can be taken as guidelines. As you proceed on life's pathway, you will learn to answer your own questions and the self-supporting inclination of life will meet all of your real needs, on time and in most appropriate ways.

When I look at social and global conditions, I don't see too much evidence that very many people are experiencing life as you say it can be experienced. How do you know that present world conditions are not the way they are supposed to be? And how can I know that I am supposed to unfold the innate capacities and abilities you talk about?

It is true that perhaps three-quarters of the global population are today living unconsciously. They are not well educated, well informed or living with high purpose. Many would like to experience improved conditions, but they don't know how to proceed. Also, many who know how to do better are self-limited because of poor self-esteem and because they do not yet know about the promise of *all things possible*. However, I am sure that most people are diligently doing their best to help themselves, and many are learning and improving. I am convinced that it is our responsibility to make the vision of possibilities more widely available and to support our extended human family in more practical ways. You can know that you are meant to unfold your innate capacities and use your creative abilities, because you want to, you aspire to do so. All that is needed is decision and commitment. Decision will focus your life and commitment will motivate you to be involved in a realistic program of study, self-examination and purposeful behavior. Your progressive psychological and spiritual growth, along with improved circumstances, will confirm what is emphasized in this book—and what you know in your heart to be true.

I am extremely interested in the possibilities you describe. More, I'm enthusiastic! But before I involve myself too deeply, I want to be able to know God's will for me. How can I be sure to take the right path in life?

Ask yourself if you are sincere, if you are willing to persist once the way is known to you and if you are really willing to know and do God's will. Then study more deeply in order to understand, at least in part, the nature of God and the purpose of your life. Let the soul yearning you have become more influential. Then, whatever you do that is selfless, nurturing, constructive, life-enhancing and entirely beneficial for yourself and others who are influenced by your actions, can be considered to be in line with God's will. This approach is for general behavior, in all that we do and in all relationships. As for knowing what it is you are specifically to do, that will be a matter of soul-searching, an evaluation of your talents and skills, and how you best feel you can serve the cause of evolution. In all relationships and actions, regardless of your chosen or destined path in life, let excellence be the ideal. Be the best you can be and do the best you can do, then offer the results to God. I believe that some souls are born with a destiny, a special purpose which is sooner or later revealed to them.

Others are born to complete unfinished business and to keep agreements made earlier. Some are here to learn how to play the game of life and prepare themselves to more consciously participate in the unfolding drama. The primary purpose for our being here is to grow spiritually. With this, understanding unfolds and grace determines.

I've tried positive thinking, goal-setting, affirmations and almost everything else I can think of, and nothing seems to work for me. I still have a difficult time changing my personal habits and accomplishing what I want to accomplish. What am I doing wrong? Better yet, what can I do to be more successful in my efforts?

If the procedures you mention "worked" unfailingly, there would be millions of fulfilled, functional people in the world today, for these procedures have been known and used for centuries. Positive thinking can be helpful, goal-setting is certainly useful, and affirmations, correctly used, can be life-transforming. But none of these procedures are effective unless a change occurs in our states of consciousness. Positive thinking is seldom result-producing while negative feelings and uncertainty about desired outcomes remain as restrictive factors. Goal-setting will have but marginal successful results if self-defeating attitudes and behaviors are allowed to persist. And affirmations, to be beneficial, must enable us to adjust attitudes and viewpoints so that we experience a shift from "wanting to be," to "being," from "wanting to have," to "having." It is helpful to use these procedures because they provide learning opportunities. But as you proceed, be reminded of the importance of how you see the world and how you see yourself in relationship to it. This will determine your purpose, your behavior, and your circumstances and general pattern of experiences. Start by changing your habits and train yourself to do what you know you should do, as duty. Submission to duty can be pleasant, because such behavior makes us feel better about ourselves. The cheerful performance of duty also soon results in the manifestation of positive benefits. To the best of your ability correct wrong (non-useful) behavior and concentrate on doing what is result-producing. With practice you will learn to live from inner confidence. Then positive thinking will be natural, goal-setting will be an act of inspiration, and your inner conversations will be entirely supportive of your high purposes.

I am a possibility-thinker and in my heart I believe in all things possible. Yet, when I envision desirable outcomes I am still aware that I am not-so-subconsciously holding onto beliefs and feelings which are contrary to what I envision as possible. I sometimes even fall into the pattern of thinking like some of my friends think, that to be human is to be subject to limitations. I want to be free and functional and I am not a selfish person. I just want to be able to do things I feel are worth doing. How should I proceed?

Go more deeply into yourself, until you feel consciously grounded in the Infinite, in the field of pure consciousness which is the realm of all possibilities. Meditate until your thought processes are refined and your awareness is temporarily withdrawn from identification with your personality. Feel yourself to be a spiritual being, completely immersed in the omnipresent, omnipotent reality of God. From this level of awareness, *gently* imagine worthwhile possibilities. Refrain from the inclination to exercise will or personal effort to force the issue. Just rest in the deep silence, firm in the realization, the knowing, that your worthy purposes are already fulfilled, already an established fact in your consciousness. After this interlude, resume your normal activities while inwardly maintaining your realized convictions. Don't analyze the creative process or discuss it with anyone else. Just know that the creative forces which make possible all outcomes are supportive of your endeavors. You may be led to do practical things to help unfold desired conclusions. If you do not know what to do, or if it seems to you that there is nothing you can do, then do nothing outwardly. Just maintain your awareness of inner certainty. You will experience intuitive insights. You will be led to spontaneously do the right things. Life itself will provide the means for the fulfillment of your worthy dreams. Learn to enjoy social relationships without being unduly influenced by the words, attitudes or behaviors of others who do not yet share your lofty vision of how life can be.

I know I should meditate and I really want to, but I don't seem to have time enough in my schedule to add another routine to my busy lifestyle. Can I meditate while attending to business and social matters? If not, what do you suggest I do?

I suggest that you be honest with yourself and decide what is important in your life. I suggest that you "make a daily appointment with God" and keep that appointment during your regularly scheduled meditation session. It is useful, of course, to be centered and soul conscious while attending to routine matters. But to meditate correctly, you will need to arrange circumstances so that you have private time alone. With all of your "busy-ness," have you seriously examined the purposes for which you do what you do? Honestly contemplate the matter and decide what is important and what is not important. Write a list of your priorities. Train yourself to be more efficient. Eliminate involvements and relationships which are not essential. Since meditation, correctly practiced, improves health and performance, it should be of major importance to you. I find, as many do, that a good time to meditate is early in the morning. Go to bed earlier in the evening, then after refreshing sleep, meditate and let your consciousness extend into the unbounded field of the Infinite. If you think about it, I'm sure you will agree that you really can schedule your life and do the many things "you really want to do."

Another question about meditation. Some of my friends tell me that they enjoy listening to music while they meditate. Some even promote the use of tape recorded subliminal suggestions for the purpose of conditioning the mind in a positive way. What do you think about these practices?

If your purpose for meditating is to experience superconscious states and awaken to a conscious awareness of your true nature, it is best to meditate in the silence. External sounds of any kind, including inspirational music, will be a distraction. Uplifting music can be enjoyed at other times, including prior to meditation if it provides inspiration and awakens devotion. Since the purpose of meditation is to experience clear states of consciousness which, in turn, have a constructive influence upon the mind, the use of subliminal recorded suggestions is not recommended. Another subtle factor is that when we listen to the spoken words of another person, especially when we are in a relaxed, receptive state of consciousness, we can also acquire attitudes and personality characteristics of the speaker. Unless I am listening to a fully enlightened person or "the voice of God Himself," I do not want such unmonitored influences invading my consciousness. Repeated superconscious episodes, however, are entirely beneficial, order thoughts in a constructive manner, and weaken and dissolve destructive drives and tendencies rooted in deeper layers of the mind. We do not want to further condition the mind by any means—we want to reduce the effects of restrictive conditionings. Inspired decision-making, intentional adjustments in mental attitude, commitment to sensible modes of behavior, and self-responsible actions are also helpful in regulating subconscious processes so that optimum function is experienced. When meditating, withdraw attention from conditioned awareness and experience, to whatever degree possible, soul awareness. This is the way to peace of mind and spiritual growth.

I'm almost desperate in my attempts to establish a meaningful, loving relationship with someone I deeply care about and who cares for me. So far, I have been unsuccessful in doing this. Will possibility-thinking and creative imagination be helpful in enabling me to fulfill this desire?

If the creative process works for one thing, it will work for another. While it may not be easy to do, first work on getting clear of your feelings of desperation. And avoid desperate behavior completely. You might also want to honestly look at your habitual attitudes, self-esteem, personality traits and behaviors, to determine whether or not some constructive changes need to be made. What you are is what you will attract in relationships. What do you have to offer in a relationship? What is the real purpose of the relationship you desire? What kind of a person are you? What kind of a person do you want to spend your life with? Are you motivated by insecurity, loneliness, peer group influences or vague yearnings, or do you honestly want to enjoy life to the full in a normal (natural) healthy-minded way? If possible, it is better to proceed from inner strength and self-sufficiency, then a mature relationship is more likely to unfold. After thinking the matter over carefully, in your imagination "see" (and be sure to *feel*) yourself happy and fulfilled. You need not, at this time, envision a specific person. How would you feel if you were happy in a relationship? What would you do? Imagine all of the possibilities. In the meantime, live a purposeful, productive life. This is the best preparation for a worthwhile relationship.

I'm confused. In some spiritual literature I read that one should eliminate personal desire. Yet you speak of planning, of accomplishing purposes and of fulfilling desired ends. What is the best way to look at the matter?

Every healthy person has urges which result in desires. We desire to know our purpose in life. We desire to have our basic needs met. We desire to express creatively. We desire to understand the meaning of life and our relationship with it. We desire to know the reality of God and to grow spiritually. These are innate desires which should be fulfilled. What is psychologically damaging and spiritually deadening is to be driven by compulsion, or to attempt to satisfy these natural urgings by means which are not fulfilling. Also, unreasonable cravings for unnecessary possessions, recognition, power, accomplishment, sensory gratification of any kind—or any other experience or circumstance which is not of lasting value—can result in the wasting of vital forces and in missing the real purpose of human life. The real purpose of human life is to become spiritually aware and to flow with the currents of evolution which contribute to the fulfillment of life's purposes. Do everything you can to contribute to your total wellness, to an open relationship with the universe, to supportive relationships, and to success in worthy ventures. Just do not be attached to results, or let your ego get in the way of the correct performance of your duties. Let your reliance be upon God, not upon externals. In this way you will learn to live easily in the world and not lose sight of important matters.

I want to be able to share with others. I want to be able to help others, but I don't have surplus resources to share. How can I give to others if my personal means are limited?

Your present personal circumstances may be modest, but as a spiritual being you are without limitation. Help others by first helping yourself to be a whole person, a spiritually aware person. In this way you will share your consciousness with the collective consciousness of the human race and with planetary consciousness. Further, share yourself by truly loving all people and by wishing them the highest and best. Envision wonderful circumstances for yourself and for everyone else. See your own possibilities and let them unfold. See the good and the possible in others and call it forth by your conscious recognition. In your relationships with members of your family, friends, and people you meet in various circumstances, be kind and considerate. This is a marvelous way to immediately share with others. If you have creative ideas which can be implemented, let them come into expression. If you have creative ideas others can use to their benefit, share them freely. If you can offer a helping hand in practical ways, do so. After you meditate, let your God-realization radiate into the mental atmosphere of the planet. Speak cheerful, encouraging words to others and in this way encourage and inspire them to improved performance. If you have any financial resources at all, begin sharing a modest amount in sensible ways. You will find that as you learn to give freely and wisely, that you are in the flow of more available resources. The universe will supply you with your every need, and more. Remember, too, that everything flows into manifestation from the unmanifest field of pure consciousness. Therefore, look to the source while learning to cooperate with the creative processes which nourish you. As you do these things, you will not only experience soul satisfaction because you are making a useful contribution to others, you will also experience steady spiritual growth. Don't wait until your circumstances are better. Open yourself to life, now. Do what you can, now. Grace flows through any open person. You will see evidence of this as you proceed with surrendered love.

What is the best way to share these ideas with young people?

The most obvious best way is to be an ideal role model, by living righteously; that is, correctly. Live like this so that your children, and young adults you know, will have an opportunity to emulate your positive qualities and behaviors while learning to find their own path in life.

When they ask questions, give them honest, accurate answers. Because they are spiritual beings, knowledge is within them and needs only opportunities to unfold. This is the education process, the bringing out of innate understanding and ability. Provide them with unlimited opportunities for learning and discovery. Do not neglect their spiritual education. Encourage them to cultivate the virtues, to be honest and moral, to choose a natural lifestyle and to maintain physical and psychological wellness. Let them know the importance of being kind to the planet and of using resources wisely. All of the things you wish you had known when you were younger, let them know. All of the opportunities you wish you had been provided, provide for them if you can. Have good literature available. Acquaint them with the arts and sciences. See to their higher learning, so they will be able to fulfill their purposes in life. Nurture them, provide a secure environment, and do them no harm. Every young person should have available the information in this book, should be taught to meditate and should have a correct, realistic understanding of God and the purpose for being in this world.

I am a reasonably functional person but I am aware of the fact that memories of past unpleasant circumstances, a few of them painful to think about, sometimes interfere with my constructive intentions and even cause me to behave inappropriately. In other words, I am aware that these memories influence me in ways which are not always beneficial. How can I eliminate these influences?

There is no unenlightened (fully God-realized) person who does not have this problem. To be spiritually liberated means to be completely soul conscious and free from unwanted mental and emotional disturbances. Sometimes, merely recalling the episodes and circumstances which resulted in traumatic or otherwise influential memories, and coming to terms with them, can release their influences. It is also helpful to be self-responsible and purposeful, understanding that the past cannot be changed but the present and future can be chosen. With learning and improved performance, unconscious and subconscious conditionings can be disarmed, their influences weakened and dissolved. The more successful we become in living with purpose, the less we are influenced by memories of the past. It is important to avoid feeling like a victim of circumstances and not to blame past circumstances, or individuals for present conditions. Feed your mind with positive influences. Associate with functional people. Cultivate attitudes and behaviors which will contribute to physical and psychological health. Attend to your spiritual practices and awaken to the fact that as a spiritual being you do not have to be unduly influenced by mental conflicts and emotional confusion. *Cultivate a total lifestyle that is fully supportive of your highest aspirations.* Be the person you can be. Let yourself grow to emotional maturity.

I am not unfolding spiritually as I would like to. How much do my personal efforts influence the spiritual growth process? How much is either predetermined or due to God's grace?

All of these factors have a bearing on our spiritual growth. Much of our spiritual growth is determined by our personal participation in the process—living in harmony with natural laws, living with conscious purpose, and attending to our spiritual practices. As we do these things, our mental processes become more refined, our emotional states become more harmonized, and the brain and nervous system become more capable of processing higher states of consciousness. We live correctly, not merely to be good human beings, but to allow vital forces which would have otherwise been used to repair the physical and psychological damage caused by wrong living, to be used to refine the body and transform the mind. There is a psychological and physiological relationship to spiritual awareness. Just as the cultivation of higher states of consciousness can beneficially influence mind and body, so a purified mind and a healthy body can allow higher states of consciousness to be experienced and expressed. This is one reason why the cultivation of constructive mental states, natural living and divine contemplation are recommended. So, personal involvement is important. Then there is a deeper process at work, the inclination of life to fulfill purposes which often determines outcomes with or without our cooperation. I would be open to this influence, while not depending entirely upon it. In other words, don't expect it to do for you what you can, and should, do for yourself. The inclination of life to fulfill purposes is the action of grace, but grace can become more pronounced in influence when we learn to be more responsive to it. For this, continue with your reasonable program to help yourself while, at the same time, learning to surrender more completely to God's will for you. In these ways you will be open to all possible helpful influences.

What is a clear, simple guideline for living?

Live with conscious purpose, discipline your mind and senses, study to learn how to function in this world and to understand the higher laws of consciousness, and trust in God.

A Final Note

I hope you have benefited by the reading of this book. I know you will continue to grow in knowledge and abound in grace. As you apply yourself with surrendered diligence to the transforming processes occurring within and around you which assure your fulfillment in the divine plan, your destiny will become increasingly known to you.

Human life is too precious, too spiritually worthwhile, to waste in confused thinking and misdirected effort. Just as every day can be an opportunity for a new beginning, so every moment can be ripe with the promise of fresh discovery. But the pure, the spiritual desire must be the prevailing factor.

You are a being of eternity. Nothing belongs to you and you belong to no one. You are here to express divinity and to transcend all limitations, even the illusion of death. Evolutional forces will work through you, to the degree that you allow them. Whatever you can know in your heart, and truly believe, is possible to you.

I acknowledge you as the bright, capable being you are.

With love,

RESOURCES

To supplement your practices and support your chosen lifestyle, the following books by Roy Eugene Davis are recommended.

An Easy Guide to Meditation

How to meditate for personal benefits and spiritual growth. The natural process anyone can use. The procedure, with techniques and recommendations. *Softcover, 128 pages, $3.00.*

How You Can Use the Technique of Creative Imagination

Specific guidelines to possibility-thinking, creative planning and purposeful visualization of worthy ideals and purposes. *Softcover, 128 pages, $3.95.*

Life Surrendered in God

A master text for persons on the awakening path. Part One includes philosophy, categories of cosmic manifestation and the essentials to support further study and practice. Part Two provides a comprehensive commentary on the *Yoga Sutras*, a teaching on concentration, meditation, contemplation and higher states of consciousness. Part Three outlines recommended lifestyle routines and meditation regimens, for beginning meditators and those more advanced. *Hardcover, 400 pages, $14.95.*

Obtain these books from your regular book source or direct from the publisher. Include $1.50 for the first book and 30 cents for each additional book, for handling and postage. A free book list is available upon request.

CSA Press, Publishers
Post Office Box 7
Lakemont, Georgia 30552
U.S.A.

Note: If outside of North America, when possible obtain these books through the established distributors listed on page 4.

CENTER FOR SPIRITUAL AWARENESS

Center for Spiritual Awareness is a new era enlightenment movement with international headquarters and retreat facility in the low mountains of northeast Georgia. Here, on an eleven acre site are the administration offices, meeting hall and dining room, meditation temple, library, and quiet guest houses for retreat participants.

Branch centers are in several U.S. cities, Europe and West Africa and trained meditation teachers offer instruction and programs in many communities.

CSA's teaching emphasis is that it is possible for every caring person, through right personal effort and God's grace, to experience a conscious relationship with God and live a mature, purposeful and fulfilled life.

A magazine, monthly lessons and other instructional materials are sent to interested persons around the world. CSA Press is the book publishing department.

Informative Literature is Available Upon Request

**Center for Spiritual Awareness
Post Office Box 7   Lake Rabun Road
Lakemont, Georgia 30552
U.S.A.**

**Share the good news
about** *All Things Possible*
with your friends

This helpful book by Roy Eugene Davis could be very meaningful to people you know. Individuals, groups and organizations are invited to request multiple copies for giving or resale. Contact the publisher for special prices.